*Popular Literature from
Nineteenth-Century France*

Popular Literature from Nineteenth-Century France

ENGLISH TRANSLATION

TRANSLATED BY

Masha Belenky and
Anne O'Neil-Henry

The Modern Language Association of America
New York   2021

MLA and the MODERN LANGUAGE ASSOCIATION are trademarks
owned by the Modern Language Association of America. For
information about obtaining permission to reprint material from MLA
book publications, send your request by mail (see address below) or
e-mail (permissions@mla.org).

Library of Congress Cataloging-in-Publication Data

Names: Belenky, Masha, 1968– translator. | O'Neil-Henry, Anne,
 translator.
Title: Popular literature from nineteenth-century France : English
 translation / translated by Masha Belenky and Anne O'Neil-Henry.
Description: New York : The Modern Language Association of
 America, 2021. | Series: Texts and translations, 1079-2538 ; 33 |
 Includes bibliographical references. | Summary: "An English
 translation of humorous works published in French for a mass
 audience. Describes the changing society of nineteenth-century
 Paris, featuring character types such as the flâneur, the grisette,
 the gamin, and the bourgeois. Includes texts by Paul de Kock,
 Honoré de Balzac, Delphine de Girardin, Louis Huart, and
 others"— Provided by publisher.
Identifiers: LCCN 2020028170 (print) | LCCN 2020028171 (e-book) |
 ISBN 9781603294966 (paperback) | ISBN 9781603294973 (EPUB) |
 ISBN 9781603294980 (Kindle edition)
Subjects: LCSH: French literature—19th century—Translations into
 English. | Popular literature—France—Translations into English.
Classification: LCC PQ1113 .P67 2021 (print) | LCC PQ1113 (e-book) |
 DDC 840.8/007—dc23
LC record available at https://lccn.loc.gov/2020028170
LC e-book record available at https://lccn.loc.gov/2020028171

Texts and Translations 33

ISSN 1079-2538

Cover illustration from Louis Huart's "Physiologie du flaneur."
Bibliothèque Nationale de France.

Published by The Modern Language Association of America
85 Broad Street, Suite 500, New York, New York 10004-2434
www.mla.org

In memory of
Priscilla Parkhurst Ferguson

CONTENTS

LIST OF ILLUSTRATIONS

All illustrations are courtesy of the Bibliothèque Nationale de France.

ACKNOWLEDGMENTS

First and foremost, we would like to thank the stellar editorial team at the MLA Texts and Translations series for their enthusiasm for this project from the start, and for expertly shepherding it through various stages of review and production. In particular, we wish to thank Jaime Cleland, Zahra Brown, and Erika Suffern. We are very grateful for the invaluable feedback from our insightful reviewers, whose astute comments and suggestions helped better this project.

We are grateful for the support of the Department of French and Francophone Studies at Georgetown University and of Georgetown College, as well as George Washington University's Columbian College of Arts and Sciences and Department of Romance, German, and Slavic Languages and Literatures. We thank Hannah Merrill, our student assistant, for her transcription work.

We thank numerous colleagues who gracefully answered our queries about various obscure aspects of French language and culture: Caroline Ferraris-Besso, Susan Hiner, Iris Smorodinsky, Kasia Stempniak, Herica Valladares, and Paul Young.

We both are very lucky to have been able to draw on the professional expertise of our parents: Mary Anne O'Neil, Patrick Henry, and Mark Belenky. As professors of French literature and a professional translator, respectively, they faithfully read and commented on drafts of our translations, caught a number of unfortunate infelicities, and no doubt greatly improved the final product.

We would like to thank our families for their unwavering support for this project.

Finally, this volume is the result of a productive and fun collaboration over the course of several years, involving translation boot camps, delicious lunches, meetings both in person and from different coasts, and many thousands of e-mails. It was a pleasure to work together, and we are both grateful for the experience.

Introduction

The day a new book by the nineteenth-century novelist Paul de Kock went on sale, "il y avait une véritable émeute en librairie" 'there was a veritable riot in bookstores' (Mirecourt 33).[1] But who was this Paul de Kock? To readers of his time, his name was as familiar as those of Stendhal, Victor Hugo, and Gustave Flaubert are to modern students of French literature. De Kock is one of many now-forgotten writers whose works were widely consumed by the bourgeois reading public and who outsold many of their now-canonical counterparts. These authors' popularity and financial success anticipated that of modern writers of genre fiction like Danielle Steel or John Grisham. The period in which they published was a liminal one: after the notion of highbrow and lowbrow literature had been established in the seventeenth century, but before literary canons were created in the late nineteenth century. These texts thus emerged from a developing literary marketplace, one in which our modern conceptions of popular culture were not yet fully articulated and in which there was much overlap between the authors who are now well known and those we no longer read. Works by canonical authors present a compelling but incomplete picture of that literary landscape and of the questions that preoccupied French society at the time. This volume showcases the rich and diverse popular literature that was so riveting to nineteenth-century readers. If the works in question were not written by and for the people—and thus not *populaire* in the French sense of the term—they were representative of the tastes of the growing bourgeois class. Reading this literature deepens and nuances our understanding of nineteenth-century French culture and society.

This anthology brings together for the first time a range of literary texts from different genres that were widely consumed and broadly disseminated but for the most part have not been reproduced in modern editions. We focus in particular on the middle decades of the nineteenth century, a time of major developments in the literary marketplace and in reading practices. The anthology includes popular authors such as de Kock, Jules Janin, Louis Huart, Delphine de Girardin, and Eugène Scribe. While each text here is representative of its particular genre and the author's distinct style, there are numerous points of connection and overlap that create a sense of cohesion and give the reader a more complete understanding of the cultural moment in which these texts were created.

Many of the texts in this anthology have not been included in the French literary canon because of their supposed lack of aesthetic quality and literary value; should today's readers therefore approach them differently than they do the works of literary giants such as Stendhal, Hugo, and Flaubert? The answer, we believe, is at once yes and no. On the one hand, we propose reading these works as any other work of literature—through careful close textual analysis informed by cultural and historical context. It is through attention to style and language, as well as analyses of rhetorical strategies, that readers of both highbrow and lowbrow literature are able to fully appreciate the nuances of a text. On the other hand, we invite readers to consider carefully the context of the period's literary marketplace and to reflect on the commercial pressures, and on the tastes of different types of readers, that ultimately drove authors to produce what became qualified as lowbrow or middlebrow literature. The works in this anthology not only provide insight into nineteenth-century social relations and details of everyday life but also reflect, and indeed shape, perceptions and ways of thinking of the period. Last but not least, we wish to point out the importance of wit in these texts. Nineteenth-century readers delighted in these works for their satire, inside jokes, irony, and topical references. Our anthology is designed to illuminate these references and to bring out their humor for contemporary readers. An understanding of what made these texts amusing is an invaluable way to unlock the mentality of nineteenth-century French society.

A Changing Literary Marketplace

The period represented in this anthology was one of major cultural shifts, both in France and across Europe, characterized, as Martina Lauster points out, by an "unprecedented expansion of ephemeral print media and graphic journalism" (2). The literature we analyze here provides examples of the emerging tastes of new consumers of culture. Many factors contributed to the profound transformation of the literary marketplace in the first half of the nineteenth century. To begin with, during this period, readership increased appreciably. Educational reforms, such as the 1833 Guizot Law, requiring an elementary school for boys in each commune, and the Falloux Law of 1850, requiring additional schools for girls, resulted in a rise of national literacy rates. By 1848, eighty-seven percent of working-class men and seventy-nine percent of working-class women were able to read, though not all these individuals were able to write.[2] Such developments allowed writers to reach a much larger reading public and, in turn, led to the emergence of professional writers who sold their books for a living (rather than being supported by a wealthy patron as before). Both authors and publishers dealt with an increasingly literate audience by developing tactics to appeal to new tastes in order to market and sell their products.

Technological innovations also dramatically changed the way books and newspapers were printed. Numerous advancements in press and paper technology enabled books to be produced and disseminated more easily and cheaply than ever before. Chief among these improvements were the introduction of mechanical presses and ink rollers, the invention of paper from wood pulp that was now produced in continuous rolls rather than sheets, and the mechanization of bookbinding. Changes affected the ways that readers learned about and accessed literary works as well. In the first decades of the nineteenth century, it was the job of sales assistants to advertise and distribute books. Eventually some sale assistants worked independently—on commission—for multiple publishers. Outside of major cities, it was traveling booksellers (*colporteurs*) who typically sold these books. Another important development was the emergence, in the eighteenth century, of lending libraries and reading rooms (*cabinets de lecture*) where readers who could not afford to purchase their own copies could have access to books or newspapers for a modest fee. In the nineteenth century, the *cabinets de lecture* flourished as a place for reading periodicals. Just as the reading public was increasing, literature was becoming more available to broader slices of the population.

Transformation of the press also played a key role in making literature more accessible to larger audiences. In 1836, two newspapers were launched at significantly lower subscription prices than other popular political dailies (forty francs instead of eighty): Emile de Girardin's *La presse* (*The*

Press) and Armand Dutacq's *Le siècle* (*The Century*). This reduced price was made possible by financing these publications through paid advertising, instead of relying entirely on subscriptions, thus rendering them more affordable. This gambit paid off, and newspaper readership increased markedly: Parisian daily papers reached up to 235,000 readers by the late 1850s. The rise of the serial novel spurred the transformation of the newspaper from a political publication to one more accessible and appealing to a general public. The name for a serial novel in French, *roman-feuilleton*, referred to the *feuilleton*, the bottom portion of the newspaper page. It was Girardin who published France's first serial novel, Balzac's *La vieille fille* (*An Old Maid*), in *The Press* in 1836—a move that in turn helped sell his paper. The most famous author of the *roman-feuilleton* of this period was Eugène Sue, whose *Les mystères de Paris* (*The Mysteries of Paris*) was published between 1842 and 1843 in the *Journal des débats* (*The Journal of Debates*). Thanks to this novel, the newspaper's subscriptions grew by the thousands. Although the *roman-feuilleton* enjoyed broad readership, the majority of its readers still belonged to the bourgeoisie, since the subscription rates of these journals were prohibitively high for working-class readers. Nonetheless, it is difficult to overstate the profound impact of the newspaper on the dynamic and symbiotic connections between the press and literature, news and fiction, authors and journalists.

In addition to social and technological forces, other factors altered the business of selling books. The new figure of the *éditeur*, or publisher, emerged during this period as a professional who was responsible for all aspects of book production: seeking out, financing, and ultimately producing and advertising books written by other authors. Moreover, publishers often introduced major innovations in the way books were formatted and printed. For example, in 1838 Gervais Charpentier launched what became known as the "format-Charpentier": full texts in smaller editions that were attractive not only to readers but to the *cabinets de lecture*, which could afford to stock more copies because of their low price. By the end of the nineteenth century, the *maisons d'édition*, or publishing houses, were established. As with other industries, the profession of publishing was shaped by a growing capitalist economy.

Like print culture, visual culture was transformed by technological innovations during this period; in particular, illustration underwent a sea change. Two advances were especially instrumental for the development of modern visual media: the advent of lithography and that of wood engraving (Mainardi 2). Lithography was first introduced at the end of the eighteenth century as a cheap way to disseminate revolutionary caricatures. Quickly and inexpensively produced and replicated, lithographs became a favored medium for representing everyday urban life. Lithography was associated with middlebrow audiences and intended for mass production and circulation.

But it was the introduction of wood engraving into the modern printing process that was particularly momentous for many works of popular literature, including those in this anthology. This innovative technology allowed a small image to be directly inserted into the text rather than be relegated to a separate page, thus completely upending traditional hierarchies of word and image. If in the past illustration had been subservient to narrative, now the image became a form of narrative in its own right, complementing, competing with, and sometimes contradicting the text within the space of the same page. The meaning of the works emerged from the dynamic interplay between word and image in popular literature as well as in the illustrated press. As Lauster reminds us, the kind of popular literature we include in this anthology "would be unthinkable without this technological advance in text-image production" (36; Mainardi 73). From changes in illustrations to those in the formatting, marketing, and sales of books, the period during which the works in our anthology emerged represented a revolutionary transformation of France's literary marketplace and the origins of modern mass culture.

A City in Flux

Much of the popular literature of the 1830s, 1840s, and 1850s emerged in response to dramatic transformations of the city of Paris. It was the emperor Napoleon III and Georges-Eugène Haussmann, the prefect of the Seine, who spearheaded the radical reconstruction and modernization of Paris beginning in the 1850s and lasting for two decades. This urban reconstruction, known as Haussmannization, was the largest in modern history. It encompassed all aspects of city planning, from building new streets and boulevards to constructing blocks of new apartment buildings, from modernizing infrastructure like water and sewer works to the creation of new parks. But the changes that would ultimately transform Paris from a medieval city into a modern metropolis began as early as the 1830s and 1840s. Indeed, historians agree that Haussmann's project did not represent a radical break from the first half of the nineteenth century but, rather, built on the developments and ideas of urban planners from that period (see Papayanis, Pinkney, Hahn). During the years of the July Monarchy, Paris was a city already on the verge of modernity. Its expanding population, crowding, congestion, and increasing pace all contributed to the fracturing of the urban experience and to a general sense of instability. In his novel *Ferragus*, Balzac notably described Paris as "cette monstrueuse merveille, étonnant assemblage de mouvements, de machines, de pensées, la ville aux cent mille romans" 'this monstrous marvel, an astonishing assemblage of movement, machines, ideas — a city of a hundred thousand novels,' characterizing Paris as complex, fragmented, and increasingly mobile (79).

The population of Paris increased considerably during the first half of the nineteenth century, especially among the working and the lower middle classes, as people flooded the capital from the provinces in search of better jobs. The overall number of inhabitants grew from 550,000 in 1800 to 700,000 in 1830 and reached one million in 1846. Patrice Higonnet notes that Paris acquired between 16,000 and 25,000 new residents every year between 1840 and 1850 (77). This influx was accompanied by an acceleration of industrial and commercial activities, as well as a considerable growth in circulation and traffic. New forms of public transportation, such as the omnibus (a precursor of the city bus), which emerged in the 1820s, contributed to a significant upturn in the number of vehicles and people on city streets. All these factors created the impression that life in Paris was speeding up. Notions of speed and change, whether real or perceived, were essential to the articulation of Parisian modernity. For Priscilla Parkhurst Ferguson, "[t]he modernity commonly ascribed to nineteenth-century Paris is rooted in this sense of movement, the perpetually unfinished provisional nature of the present and the immense change" (35). Such modernization was happening not just in the streets of Paris, inundated with people and vehicles, but also in the works of contemporary writers.

The physical transformation of Paris was accompanied by fundamental changes in traditional social hierarchies that had been upended by the French Revolution of 1789. The nineteenth century was a period of turmoil in France: the country was ruled by two monarchies, two empires, and three republics, and experienced two subsequent revolutions, a coup d'état, and several other uprisings.[3] Major changes in France's social and economic fabric accompanied this political upheaval. In the new capitalist industrial economy, money, not parentage, determined social status. The bourgeois class thus became a central economic, political, and cultural force. These social changes were evident in the new topography of Paris. The Chaussée d'Antin, for example, was inhabited by the nouveaux riches and the banking elite, while the fashionable Faubourg Saint-Germain belonged to the ancien régime aristocracy, and the neighborhood of Notre-Dame-de-Lorette to the prostitutes and working-class women. One's social class was determined by the neighborhood where one lived. Yet if the geographical boundaries between these urban areas became inevitably blurred by the increasing mobility throughout the city, the boundaries between different social groups also grew more porous. Scholars have long argued that the literary tastes of this period reflected a desire to understand and negotiate these shifts and, specifically, that the prevalence of typological descriptions and urban observations in popular productions attempted to make sense of new cultural codes (see Lyon-Caen, *Lecture*). Many of the texts in this anthology reflect this anxiety about social instability.

Panoramic Literature

One response to anxiety about changing urban and social structures was the emergence of "panoramic literature," a term coined retrospectively by the cultural theorist Walter Benjamin to describe the literature that aimed to represent and make sense of the city and bourgeois society in transition (33). Panoramic literature attracted a wide readership and became the hallmark of the mass literary market during the middle decades of the nineteenth century. These works sought to describe and classify the minute material details of everyday life by providing a seemingly objective, encyclopedic overview of the city, its inhabitants, and contemporary urban practices and trends. Panoramic literature came in different formats aimed at somewhat different audiences.

The widely popular *physiologies*, for example, were cheap, pocket-sized volumes made for quick and easy consumption that examined individual urban social types or specific Parisian phenomena. About 120 of these humorous sketches were published between 1840 and 1842, and approximately 500,000 copies were printed during this period (Sieburth 163). The Maison Aubert, a publishing house run by Gabriel Aubert and Charles Philipon that also produced lithographic prints, caricatures, and the well-known satirical journals *La caricature* and *Le charivari*, was one of the main producers of these works. Most *physiologies* were illustrated by well-known artists of the time, such as Paul Gavarni, Henry Monnier, and Honoré Daumier, adding to the works' appeal. The titles, such as *Physiologie du flâneur* (*Physiology of the Flâneur*),[4] *Physiologie de la grisette* (*Physiology of the Grisette*), and *Physiologie du tailleur* (*Physiology of the Tailor*), evoked the emerging scientific discipline of physiology. Yet in their approach to contemporary phenomena, these works employed a literary and pseudosociological style rather than a scientific one.[5] Most *physiologies* followed a prescribed formula dictating structure, length, and style. The satiric *Physiologie des physiologies* self-reflexively pokes fun at the entire genre to which it belongs by proposing the following definition of *physiologie*: "Ce mot se compose de deux mots grecs, dont la signification est désormais celle-ci: Volume in-18; composé de 124 pages, et d'un nombre illimité de vignettes, de culs de lampes, de sottises et de bavardage à l'usage des gens niais de leur nature" 'The term is composed of two Greek words, and it means the following: published in the in-18 format; composed of 124 pages, and of any number of vignettes, of cul-de-lampes, of silly mistakes, and of chitter-chatter both done by people ignorant by nature' (43).[6] Within this formula, however, the *physiologies* also included a remarkable variety of styles, often blending vignettes, dialogues, and descriptive passages. A satirical genre known for mocking contemporary mores, the *physiologies* offered remarkable insight into the social dynamics of the time while also providing the middle classes with a space for self-reflection.

Panoramic literature came both in inexpensive formats like the *physiologies*, which cost only one franc each, and in pricier ones such as the literary guidebooks known as *tableaux de Paris* (Ferguson 55). These books were sold either in installments or in bound editions that targeted more affluent readers. Examples of the literary guidebooks include the collectively authored *Paris, ou le livre des cent-et-un* (1831–34; *Paris; or, the Book of a Hundred and One*), *Les Français peints par eux-mêmes* (1840–42; *The French Depicted by Themselves*), and numerous other volumes titled *Nouveaux tableaux de Paris* (*New Panoramas of Paris*). Like the *physiologies*, the luxury volumes contained vignettes depicting everyday urban phenomena (types, events, places, professions), yet their structure and style were less formulaic. Contributors to these works wrote in a wide variety of genres: short stories, dialogues, essays, and straight typological descriptions as those found in the *physiologies.*[7] These texts owe their commercial success not only to their humorous style and lavish illustrations but also to the careful publicity campaigns launched by their publishers. Many *physiologies* contained references to other volumes in the series as well as to the publishing houses that produced them. Louis Huart's *Physiology of the Flâneur*, for instance, features an illustration of a flâneur intently gazing at the caricatures in the window of the very Aubert shop in which this *physiologie* was published and sold. Because the flâneur is so riveted by what he sees in the shop, he is unaware that he is being robbed by a pickpocket. This type of in-text advertising, coupled with the many ads for the *physiologies* that could be found in the mass press during this period, ensured the popularity of these short works.

The panoramic literary texts enabled nineteenth-century readers to navigate and comprehend their constantly changing society. They provided tools for classifying and understanding social and cultural codes during a moment of great upheaval. If for Benjamin these texts epitomized the lowbrow tastes of the period, recent scholars have argued that, instead, they represented a "dynamism of the text-image relationship" characteristic of the new journalistic media (Lauster 4). For today's readers, these complex works offer a window into the ways in which the nineteenth-century bourgeois public grappled with a society in transition. While these works are on the whole heavily inflected with the class and gender biases of their authors, they nonetheless offer key insight into the preoccupations and anxieties of nineteenth-century France.

Anthology Overview

We have included a variety of representative popular texts belonging to different genres by authors who would have been highly recognizable to their reading public: de Kock, Huart, Balzac, Janin, and Scribe, among others. The anthology is organized chronologically and addresses many of the same themes—class mobility, changing gender roles, the transformation of urban spaces, and the place of money and social status—that canonical authors of the period also explored. Such popular works were not exclusive to the first half of the nineteenth century; literary guidebooks like Edmond Texier's *Tableau de Paris* (1852; *Panorama of Paris*) or the multiauthored *Paris-Guide par les principaux écrivains et artistes de la France* (1867; *Paris Guide by the Principal Writers and Artists of France*) appeared well into the Second Empire. We have chosen to focus on the middle decades of the century, however, because these works came out of and exemplified the changing political, social, and urban moment as well as the new publishing context. Readers will likely notice that only two of the authors included here, Eugénie Foa and Delphine de Girardin, are women. As many scholars have noted, women writers produced important work and gained increased visibility during this period. However, opportunities were still limited for them, and male authors dominated the literary market (see Cohen, *Sentimental Education*; Nesci).

We begin with three selections from *Paris; or, The Book of a Hundred and One*, an influential multivolume literary guidebook published between 1831 and 1834 and collectively authored by one hundred and one writers. The book included sketches of types ("Le bourgeois de Paris" ["The Parisian Bourgeois"], "Le bibliomane" ["The Bibliomaniac"]), places ("Les bibliothèques publiques" ["Public Libraries"], "La morgue" ["The Morgue"]), and Parisian phenomena ("Un voyage en omnibus" ["An Omnibus Journey"], "Une première représentation" ["An Opening Night"]), as well as essays on more esoteric topics such as "Le marchand de chien" ("The Dog Seller") or the history of bearded men. These highly contemporary depictions sought to provide a comprehensive view of the city and its inhabitants. *Paris; or, The Book of a Hundred and One* was instrumental in popularizing descriptions of contemporary everyday life and would later be emulated in the *physiologies* of the 1840s. Conceived in order to save the publisher, Pierre-François Ladvocat, from impending financial ruin, this lucrative project not only breathed new life into Ladvocat's business but also, more important, inaugurated a new style of book. Ladvocat writes in the preface,

> Voici donc un livre neuf, s'il en fut jamais; neuf
> par la matière, neuf par la forme, neuf par le
> procédé de la composition qui en fait une espèce
> d'encyclopédie des idées contemporaines, le
> monument d'une jeune et brillante époque,
> l'album d'une littérature ingénieuse et puissante.

> This is a new book if ever there was one; new
> in its content, new in its form, new in the
> method of its composition, which makes it a
> kind of encyclopedia of contemporary ideas,
> the monument to a young and brilliant era, an
> album of inventive and powerful literature.

Our selection includes an essay by Janin, a well-known journalist and literary and theater critic, entitled "Asmodée" ("Asmodeus"), which serves as an introduction to *Paris; or, The Book of a Hundred and One* as a whole. Janin details the history of the study of manners through satire and spells out the innovative nature of the collection. Next, Gustave d'Outrepont's "Le gamin de Paris" ("The Gamin of Paris") describes the figure of the mischievous boy who became the embodiment of the revolutionary spirit. The street urchin is memorably depicted in Eugène Delacroix's painting *La liberté guidant le peuple* (1830; *Liberty Leading the People*) and in the character of Gavroche in Hugo's *Les Misérables* (1862), but it is in d'Outrepont's text that this type is explored in depth. Our final selection from *Paris; or, The Book of a Hundred and One* is "La femme à la mode et la femme élégante en 1833" ("The Fashionable Woman and the Elegant Woman in 1833"), in which Foa describes the fleeting nature of fashionability. In addition to painting a witty portrait of Parisian high society, Foa offers incisive comments on shifting class hierarchies in a society increasingly governed by money.

Next, we include a vaudeville play from the prolific playwright Eugène Scribe: *Le fils de l'agent de change* (*The Stockbroker's Son*). Vaudeville theater was by far the most popular form of public entertainment in Paris during the first half of the nineteenth century, and Scribe came to epitomize this bourgeois-domestic genre. The *comédie-vaudeville* was concerned with capturing Paris at its most modern, and vaudeville playwrights were particularly interested in representing the everyday conflicts of social life. Under the guise of slapstick comedy, vaudeville plays often exposed underlying anxieties of the emerging commercial middle class. Scribe's 1837 play, cowritten with Henri Dupin and produced during the height of vaudeville's popularity, features a comic plot and is replete with the intertextual references and funny songs typical of the genre.

The play is followed by a selection from Girardin's *Lettres parisiennes par vicomte de Launay* (*Parisian Letters by the Vicomte de Launay*). A poet, playwright, journalist, and salonnière, Girardin enjoyed tremendous popularity at mid-century. Between 1836 and 1848, she wrote a weekly urban chronicle in *The Press*, a daily newspaper published by her husband Emile de Girardin. Written under the pseudonym Charles de Launay, her chronicle appeared in what was called the *rez-de-chaussée*, the bottom section of the newspaper. Unlike the *haut-de-page* (top of the page), devoted to political news and opinions, the *rez-de-chaussée* contained serialized fiction, society gossip, and cultural news. In her witty and perceptive column, Girardin covered a wide variety of topics, from social commentary and the study of manners to fashion and description of noteworthy cultural events such as theater premieres and art exhibits.[8] An astute observer, Girardin offered insightful snapshots of everyday Parisian life. The letter included in this anthology (from 30 November 1839) exemplifies Girardin's playful style and wit.

A short story, "Un bal de grisettes" ("A Grisette Party"), from an 1837 collection entitled *Mœurs parisiennes* (*Parisian Manners*), provides a good example of writing by the wildly popular de Kock. De Kock, whose career spanned most of the nineteenth century, was considered the quintessential petit bourgeois writer, adored by his readers and panned by many critics. A major player in the nineteenth-century Parisian literary scene, this exceptionally prolific writer produced scores of vaudevilles, novels, songs, and short stories. In 1842 alone, at least seventeen titles were listed under his name in the *Bibliographie de la France* (*Bibliography of France*; see Lyons, "Les best-sellers"; Martin and Martin). By the 1840s, de Kock, like Victor Hugo, could reliably be counted upon to sell out a print run of 2,500 copies, a significant number for this time. For comparison, Balzac, an author much better known to readers today, would normally sell only around 1,500 copies of a single edition.

We then include excerpts from another famous literary guidebook, *Les Français peints par eux-mêmes: Encyclopédie morale du dix-neuvième siècle* (*The French Depicted by Themselves: A Moral Encyclopedia of the Nineteenth Century*), a large and expensive illustrated multivolume work that promised to examine all French social types, published between 1840 and 1842. Like *Paris; or, The Book of a Hundred and One*, this illustrated work boasted contributions by many now-canonical authors, such as Balzac and Théophile Gautier; popular novelists, such as Frédéric Soulié; and journalists, such as Janin. As its subtitle suggests, this book offers a comprehensive study of a broad range of contemporary social types, reflecting the nineteenth-century tendency to classify, catalogue, and thereby control the changing social environment. The selections we include, such as Auguste de Lacroix's "Le flâneur" and Balzac's "La femme comme il faut" ("The Proper Woman"), feature social types that became central to the nineteenth-century mythology of Paris and that recur throughout numerous texts and genres of the period. The flâneur, a man of leisure who wandered about town observing and interpreting crowds, was perhaps the quintessential embodiment of modernity, made famous by Charles Baudelaire later in the century. Numerous Balzacian protagonists like Auguste de Maulincour of *Ferragus* and Henri de Marsay of *La fille aux yeux d'or* (*The Girl with the Golden Eyes*) are themselves examples of flâneurs. In "The

Proper Woman," Balzac picks up on themes already evoked in Foa's essay and presents a portrait of a distinctly modern character: "the proper woman," one who is the product of shifting social hierarchies in postrevolutionary France. Our final section continues the study of popular social types as explored in the genre of the *physiologie*. The three texts from which we provide excerpts here—*Physiology of the Grisette* and *Physiology of the Flâneur*, both by Louis Huart, and *Physiology of the Bourgeois*, by Monnier—were among the best known of the *physiologies* produced during this period. Taken together, these *physiologies* show how familiar urban types were recycled throughout and refigured in different generic formats. Though each work reflects its own vision of the grisette, the flâneur, and the bourgeois, alongside the other representations, they contribute to the creation of a mythology.

All the literature featured here is exemplary of the vibrant, rich, and witty literary culture of the mid nineteenth century. Though these works may not be as familiar to contemporary readers as those of their canonical counterparts, they were consumed widely by the growing reading public at the time of their publication and share overlapping themes and concerns with the major literary figures who are taught and studied today. Reasserting their importance in the mass marketplace in which they appeared makes possible a new understanding of nineteenth-century literary culture.

Notes

1. All translations are ours unless otherwise attributed.
2. On literacy rates see Martyn Lyons (*Readers*) and James Smith Allen.
3. Over the course of the century, France experienced the following regime changes: First Empire (1804–1814); Restoration (1814–1830); July

Monarchy (1830–1848); Second Republic (1848–1852); Second Empire (1852–1870); Third Republic (1870–1940).

4. According to Priscilla Parkhurst Ferguson, in the early nineteenth century, when the word *flâneur* first began to emerge, it appeared without the circumflex. The early iterations of this urban personage had almost universally negative connotations of a lazy idler. However, the flâneur soon changed both connotation and spelling. Ferguson writes, "But the term soon climbs the lexicographical and social ladder. The circumflex accent that the word usually acquires signals a redefinition through a change of perspective. Instead of prompting a negative moral judgement, the flâneur's conspicuous inaction comes to be taken as positive evidence of both social status and superior thought" (82–83). *Physiologie du flaneur* must have appeared on the cusp of this transition.

5. The physiologies of the 1840s had as their precursors some earlier works published in the late 1820s and early 1830s. Although these works had the word *physiologie* in their title, they did not conform to the formula typical of the 1840s production. In particular, three works are considered as forerunners of the craze for *physiologies*: Jean Anthelme Brillat-Savarin's 1825 *Physiologie du goût* (*Physiology of Taste*), Balzac's 1829 *Physiologie du mariage* (*Physiology of Marriage*), and the illustrated 1832 *Physiologie de la poire* (*Physiology of the Pear*), a work published on the heels of Philipon and Daumier's famous caricatures of King Louis-Philippe as a pear.

6. "In-18" refers to the octodecimo format, which was much smaller and therefore much cheaper than the more standard octavo format (in-8).

7. Margaret Cohen coined the term *heterogenicity* to describe the style of panoramic literature—a wide diversity of genres contained within the same text ("Panoramic Literature," 232).

8. Cheryl Morgan argues that Girardin engaged in "travestissement littéraire" 'cross-dressed literary flânerie' (59).

Works Cited

Allen, James Smith. *Popular French Romanticism: Authors, Readers and Books in the Nineteenth Century.* Syracuse UP, 1981.

Balzac, Honoré de. "La femme comme il faut." *Les Français,* vol. 1, pp. 25–32.

———. *Ferragus.* 1833. *Histoire des treize,* Garnier-Flammarion, 1988.

Benjamin, Walter. "Paris, Capital of the Nineteenth Century." *The Writer of Modern Life: Essays on Charles Baudelaire*, by Benjamin, edited by Michael W. Jennings, translated by Howard Eiland et al., Harvard UP, 2006, pp. 30–45.

Chartier, Roger, and Henri-Jean Martin, editors. *Le temps des éditeurs: Du romantisme à la Belle Époque (1830–1900)*. *Histoire de l'édition française*, edited by Martin and Chartier, vol. 3, Promodis, 1985.

Cohen, Margaret. "Panoramic Literature and the Invention of Everyday Genres." *Cinema and the Invention of Modern Life*, edited by Leo Charney and Vanessa Schwartz, U of California P, 1995, pp. 227–52.

———. *The Sentimental Education of the Novel*. Princeton UP, 1999.

d'Outrepont, Gustave. "Le gamin de Paris." *Paris*, vol. 7, pp. 121–42.

Ferguson, Priscilla Parkhurst. *Paris as Revolution: Writing the Nineteenth-Century City*. U of California P, 1994.

Foa, Eugénie. "La femme à la mode et la femme élégante en 1833." *Paris*, vol. 11, pp. 273–81.

Les Français peints par eux-mêmes: Encyclopédie morale du dix-neuvième siècle. L. Curmer, 1840–1842. 10 vols.

Girardin, Delphine de. "Lettre XXVII." *Lettres parisiennes du vicomte de Launay*, edited by Anne Martin-Fugier, vol. 1, Mercure de France, 1986, pp. 555–62.

Hahn, H. Hazel. *Scenes of Parisian Modernity: Culture and Consumption in the Nineteenth Century*. Palgrave, 2009.

Higonnet, Patrice. *Paris: Capital of the World*. Harvard UP, 2002.

Huart, Louis. *Physiologie de la grisette*. Illustrated by Paul Gavarni, Aubert, 1841.

———. *Physiologie du flaneur*. Illustrated by Alophe et al., Aubert, 1841.

Janin, Jules. "Asmodée." *Paris*, vol. 1, pp. 1–15.

Kock, Paul de. "Un bal de grisettes." *Mœurs parisiennes*, Gustave Barba, 1839, pp. 257–76.

Lacroix, Auguste de. "Le flâneur." *Les Français*, vol. 3, pp. 65–72.

Ladvocat, Pierre-François. "Avis au lecteur." *Paris*, vol. 1, pp. v–xiv.

Lauster, Martina. *Sketches of the Nineteenth Century: European Journalism and its Physiologies, 1830–1850*. Palgrave Macmillan, 2007.

Lyon-Caen, Judith. *La lecture et la vie: Les usages du roman au temps de Balzac*. Editions Tallandier, 2006.

Lyons, Martyn. "Les best-sellers." Chartier and Martin, pp. 369–97.

———. *Readers and Society in Nineteenth-Century France: Workers, Women, Peasants.* Palgrave, 2001.

Mainardi, Patricia. *Another World: Nineteenth-Century Illustrated Print Culture.* Yale UP, 2017.

Martin, Henri-Jean, and Odile Martin. "Le monde des éditeurs." Chartier and Martin, pp. 159–215.

Mirecourt, Eugène de. *Paul de Kock.* Gustave Havard, 1856.

Monnier, Henry. *Physiologie du bourgeois.* Illustrated by Monnier, Aubert, 1841.

Morgan, Cheryl. "Les chiffons de la M(éd)use: Delphine Gay de Girardin, journaliste." *Romantisme*, vol. 85, 1994, pp. 57–66.

Nesci, Catherine. *Le flâneur et les flâneuses: Les femmes et la ville à romantique.* Ellug, 2007.

Papayanis, Nicholas. *Paris before Haussmann.* Johns Hopkins UP, 2004.

Paris, ou le livre des cent-et-un. Ladvocat, 1831–34. 15 vols.

Physiologie des physiologies. Desloges, 1841.

Pinkney, David. *Decisive Years in France 1840–1847.* Princeton UP, 1986.

Scribe, Eugène, and Henri Dupin. *Le fils d'un agent de change: Comédie-vaudeville en un acte.* Marchant, 1837.

Sieburth, Richard. "Same Differences: The French *Physiologies* 1840–1842." *Notebooks in Cultural Analysis*, vol. 1, Duke UP, 1984, pp. 163–99.

Suggestions for Further Reading

Belenky, Masha. *Engine of Modernity: The Omnibus and Urban Culture in Nineteenth-Century Paris.* Manchester UP, 2019.

Boutin, Aimée. "The Flâneur and the Senses." Editorial. *Rethinking the Flâneur: Flânerie and the Senses,* special issue of *Dix-Neuf: Journal of the Society of Dix-Neuviémistes,* edited by Boutin, vol. 16, no. 2, July 2012, pp. 124–32.

Giacchetti, Claudine. *Delphine de Girardin la muse de juillet.* L'Harmattan, 2004.

Haynes, Christine. *Lost Illusions.* Harvard UP, 2010.

Lhéritier, Andrée. "*Les physiologies*: Catalogue des collections de la Bibliothèque nationale." *Étude de Presse,* vol. 9, no. 17, 1957, pp. 13–58.

Lyon-Caen, Judith. "Saisir, décrire, déchiffrer: Les mises en texte du social sous la monarchie de Juillet." *Revue Historique,* vol. 306, fasc. 2 (630), Apr. 2004, pp. 301–30.

Lyons, Martyn. *A History of Reading and Writing in the Western World.* Palgrave, 2010.

Marcus, Sharon. *Apartment Stories: City and Home in Nineteenth-Century Paris and London.* U of California P, 1999.

O'Neil-Henry, Anne. *Mastering the Marketplace: Popular Literature in Nineteenth-Century France.* U of Nebraska P, 2017.

Preiss, Nathalie. *Les physiologies en France au XIXe siècle.* Editions Inter-Universitaires, 1999.

Saint-Amand, Denis, and Valérie Stiénon. "Lectures littéraires du document physiologique: Méthodes et perspectives." *Methis,* vol. 2, 2009, pp. 71–85.

Stiénon, Valérie. *La littérature des physiologies: Sociopoétique d'un genre romantique, 1830–1845.* Classiques Garnier, 2012.

Stierle, Karlheinz. "Baudelaire and the Tradition of the Tableau de Paris." *New Literary History,* vol. 11, no. 2, Winter 1980, pp. 345–61.

Terni, Jennifer. "A Genre for Early Mass Culture: French Vaudeville and the City, 1830–1848." *Theater Journal,* vol. 58, no. 2, May 2006, pp. 221–48.

Thérenty, Marie-Eve. *Mosaïques: Être écrivain entre presse et roman (1829–1836).* Champion, 2003.

Thompson, Victoria. *The Virtuous Marketplace: Women and Men, Money and Politics in Paris, 1830–1870.* Johns Hopkins UP, 2000.

Weschler, Judith. *A Human Comedy: Physiognomy and Caricature in Nineteenth-Century Paris.* U of Chicago P, 1982.

Note on the Translations

The translations are based on original editions of French texts. While some modern French editions do exist, these works have not been presented together or translated into English.

The challenge of translating texts written over 150 years ago is to avoid making them sound anachronistic, while at the same time rendering them readable and lively to modern audiences. Our aim is to have these nineteenth-century popular texts come alive without losing the specificity of the time and place in which they were written. The works included in this volume were page-turners at the time of their publication—in other words, they were popular in all senses of the word. We hope our translation conveys this readability and the excitement these texts generated.

Tone and register can sometimes get lost in translation. This is particularly true when dealing with nineteenth-century popular literature. Indeed, much of the pleasure of reading these texts derives from their irony, insider's jokes, period-specific puns, and juxtapositions of tone and register. For example, one might find a straightforward description of a phenomenon followed by a much more whimsical section. For another, one might find references to Parisian institutions—from prisons to cafés—that would be easily recognizable to nineteenth-century French readers and have a humorous effect, but require glossing for contemporary readers. We have endeavored to convey the comic effect of many of these texts that attracted so many nineteenth-century readers without losing sight of the often astonishing depth of their sociological observations.

The works in this anthology draw on an overlapping set of themes and types and exhibit intertexual and specific cultural references that are recycled throughout this corpus. For example, the figure of Robert Macaire—a swindler—earned his own installment in the *physiologie* series, but references to him abound in other works. If these works share common content, they nevertheless each have a distinct style which we sought to preserve in the translation.

Some terms found in these works, such as *flâneur, gamin, grisette,* and *rentier,* are nineteenth-century neologisms, pregnant with cultural meaning that a literal translation would fail to convey. Having no direct equivalent in English, these words have instead been adopted into the language. Another such word is *arrondissement,* which refers to administrative districts within Paris; our footnotes often locate the places mentioned in the text within one of the twenty arrondissements that exist today. (The first twelve arrondissements were introduced in 1795, but those now in use were established in the 1850s, after the texts here were written.)

This volume contains references to different types of currency: the livre, the franc, and the sou. The livre was an old French monetary unit worth approximately 100 centimes. It was eventually replaced by the franc. The sou was a smaller unit, worth 5 centimes.

This anthology includes the work of a variety of authors—both canonical and now forgotten—who contributed to popular literature during this period. This multiplicity of authors means that the translator must convey stylistic differences. Instead of homogenizing the style, we have worked to showcase each text's narrative voice. For example, Janin's erudite "Asmodeus" and Balzac's belletristic "A Proper

Woman" are quite distinct from de Kock's dialogue-based short story or Foa's lighthearted social commentary.

Other challenges are specific to certain works. For example, the rhymed songs and lively, fast-paced dialogue of vaudeville contributed to the genre's popularity but are somewhat difficult to translate. We have sought to replicate the energy of such theatrical works.

Finally, on a more general note, whereas we may have glossed cultural references in the French version of this volume, in some cases we opted to convey the cultural context through the translation itself, using what translators call "an invisible footnote." For example, a reference to Bicêtre in Janin's "Asmodeus" is explained in a footnote in French. But in English, we simply translated it as "the Bicêtre mental asylum." Additionally, when a French text contained an idiomatic expression, we sought to find a rough equivalent in English. For example, in *The Stockbroker's Son*, Scribe uses the French proverb "C'est le greffier de Vaugirard, il ne peut écrire quand on le regarde," a rhyming saying that literally means, "It's the clerk of Vaugirard, he cannot write while being watched." We used a modified version of the English saying "a watched pot never boils." In doing so, our goal was to make these works as readable as they were for the nineteenth-century public.

Footnotes original to the texts are marked with an asterisk; numbered notes are our own. For bibliographic information on works cited in the notes, please refer to "Works Cited in Headnotes and Footnotes" at the end of the volume.

Popular Literature from
Nineteenth-Century France

Jules Janin

Asmodeus

From *Paris; or,*
The Book of a Hundred and One

In this introductory essay to Paris, ou le livre des cent-et-un *(Paris; or, The Book of a Hundred and One), Janin provides a genealogy of urban observation, broadly conceived, and a study of manners by way of the figure of Asmodeus (Asmodée), a rather benevolent king of demons who first made his appearance in the popular 1707 novel* Le diable boiteux *(The Devil upon Two Sticks), by Alain-René Lesage. Lesage's demon, typically depicted with a crooked back and a cane, explores the city of Madrid and the everyday life of its inhabitants by removing rooftops and peeking inside people's homes. References to this figure appear frequently in works written after Lesage's novel, most notably in Louis-Sébastien Mercier's* Tableau de Paris *(1781–1788; Panorama of Paris), a work that also served as a key precursor to* Paris; or, The Book of a Hundred and One. *Lesage's character thus provided a literary model for the project of* Paris; or, The Book of a Hundred and One *and for panoramic literature as a whole. In fact, the book was initially supposed to be titled* Le diable boiteux à Paris *(The Devil upon Two Sticks in Paris). Like the publisher, Pierre-François Ladvocat, in his preface, Janin seeks both to highlight the innovative nature of the new book and to situate it in the tradition of Mercier and other writers interested in social commentary. Throughout his essay, Janin refers to great works of literature and writers of previous centuries who practiced social satire.*

Where is this Asmodeus? Who will return him to us?
You, angel or demon, when will you be back to guide
us along this long road of modern manners, manners
shaped by two revolutions?[1] Oh, dear reader, you who
see the world as it is, austere, calm, poised, and melan-
cholic; do you believe that Asmodeus is possible in such
a world? Will he be at ease in this monotonous world?
Will he find enough variety and disorder in this comedy
of the everyday, not so much to applaud it but to take the
trouble to hiss at it?

When Asmodeus first appeared, things were good.
People behaved in a Spanish way, even in France. Full of
love and duels, life was enhanced, all colorfully decked
out, and was all about comedy and storytelling. Everywhere, inside and out, you could find pleasant vagaries
of opinions, of needs, of desires; this was still the world
of students, moneylenders, love, devotion, soldiers, silly
ladies, old women confessing their love, absurd doctors,
magistrates in black robes, princes in disguise, lecherous
monks, giddy widows, famous actors, poor poets, and
cuckolded husbands.[2] You can see how Asmodeus the
devil must have liked living in that world. Comedy was

---

[1] A reference to the Revolution of 1789 and the July Revolution of
1830.
[2] Stock characters from eighteenth-century adventure novels and
theater.

everywhere then, enjoyable and joyous comedy with a libertine plot. Comedy climbed upon the judge's bench, having donned his official hat, and stuck her tongue out at the litigants. Comedy sat upon a king's throne, poking fun at despotism and playing with sovereign power as one plays with a tamed tiger. Satirical Comedy had no respect for either men or things; she went up to the altar with the priest in vestments; she got drunk in the sacristy with a tipsy monk; she fought and made love in a tavern with an inebriated alguacil;[3] licentious and flighty goddess, Comedy ran through the hospital, thrashing both patient and doctor; sometimes wearing rags and a saddlebag, she evoked Diogenes the cynic;[4] other times, Comedy was a perfumed courtesan nonchalantly awaiting gallant gentlemen and fierce soldiers in her boudoir. Then, too, she was a lady of the night waiting at the corner, a secondhand clothing dealer at the stalls, a reseller of toiletries and clothes, surrounded by creams, makeup, old perfumes, used liveries, rumpled dresses, hoping to cash in on these leftovers of passions, of flirtations, of feminine luxury and destitution. Comedy performed all these jobs.

How many times did Comedy disguise herself as a censor or a police spy, never rejecting even the most

---

[3] A high-ranking officer of justice in Spain.
[4] A Greek philosopher and one of the founders of Cynicism.

embarrassing costumes? She would spend entire days at the door of a casino or a brothel—spying, watching, taking notes, wallowing in the mud.

To understand such manners, which applied equally in the king's palace and the hospice for the Incurables, in the Académie Française[5] and the mental asylum, you must understand that Comedy and commentary on manners had to be charming and animated. When Asmodeus was unleashed into a world thus made, he must have kept himself happy and proud. So watch him run, that nasty devil! Watch him walk lightly on rooftops, because at that time people had the precious advantage of being able to walk on rooftops! I imagine that the devil must have jumped up and down with joy in this colorful world of passions and vices. But alas, alas! In our polite and orderly world of proper comportment, under our drab and melancholy skies, at the height of our wisdom, what is the devil to do? The devil will die of boredom!

He's an old one, this devil! He has seen everything since society was first corrupted! He has witnessed so

---

[5] The Académie Française, or French Academy, is the most prestigious literary academy in France. It was established by Cardinal Richelieu, chief minister to Louis XIII, in 1635. Its original purpose was to maintain standards of literary taste and the purity of the French language. It consists of forty members, or *immortels*, drawn from among the most recognised writers of the time. To be elected to the Académie Française has been considered the greatest honor for a writer.

many declines! He has warned of so many disorders! He has mocked so many quirks! The devil Asmodeus, that is, the devil of observation, the one who cares about the study of manners—don't think he was born yesterday, that impish and playful child, who follows or precedes *Gil Blas* in order to explain it or to complete it.[6] Asmodeus is as old as the world. He has not always had a crooked back and a cane, and he has not always walked with a limp; he has not always been trapped in a jar;[7] he has not always been called simply Asmodeus. Over time he has assumed the following names: Aristophanes, Theophrastus, Terence, La Bruyère, and above all Molière; then he became Voltaire, Rabelais, and Beaumarchais.[8] He was

---

[6] *Gil Blas* is a picaresque novel by Alain-René Lesage, published in four volumes between 1715 and 1735.

[7] In Lesage's *The Devil upon Two Sticks*, Asmodeus is rescued from an enchanted glass bottle by a Spanish student. Following the rescue, Asmodeus joins the student on a series of adventures.

[8] Aristophanes: playwright and author of comedies in ancient Athens; Theophrastus: Greek philosopher and author of the first known collection of character sketches; Terence (Publius Terentius Afer): playwright in the Roman republic; Jean de La Bruyère: seventeenth-century French philosopher and satiric moralist especially known for his work *Les caractères* (*The Characters*), loosely inspired by Theophrastus; Molière (Jean-Baptiste Poquelin): seventeenth-century French playwright, one of the most famous French authors of comedies. Voltaire (François-Marie Arouet): an Enlightenment writer and philosopher; Pierre-Augustin Caron de Beaumarchais: an eighteenth-century French playwright particularly known for *Le barbier de Seville* (*The Barber of Seville*) and *Le mariage de Figaro* (*The Marriage of Figaro*); François Rabelais: one of the central figures of French humanism,

known by the greatest names in the world of poetry and satire. He has achieved two extremes of human genius: he had Rabelais's wit and Montaigne's heart.[9] Asmodeus is the philosophy of all times, one that can be summed up by a caricature. Asmodeus is the wisdom of antiquity translated into French. Asmodeus is the laughter of yesteryear that becomes distorted. He is reason that becomes satire, sublime and poor reason, dumbed down so as to be understood by others. But, whether he is wise or foolish, let's pay our respects to Lesage's demon. He has been exploring humankind for a long while. The first people he met in his travels were the Greeks—chatty, stubborn, crabby, epicurean, skeptical, witty, mocking, flighty, soulless. But at the same time they were flowery, pretty, polite, elegant, full of laughter, idle (especially in public places), eloquent, musical, rhetorical, enamored of form, of sounds, of colors, of smells, of poetry. But also they were vain, crass, mean, shameless, insolent. The Greeks were without a doubt a fascinating people to study—Alcibiade[10] and Gnathon[11] all at once. Ani-

---

author of the satirical series of novels *Gargantua et Pantagruel* (*Gargantua and Pantagruel*).

[9] Michel de Montaigne was a French philosopher of the Renaissance and author of the *Essais* (*Essays*).

[10] A Greek orator and statesman.

[11] A character in La Bruyère's *The Characters*, a deeply egocentric and self-absorbed man.

mated people! Asmodeus managed to depict all facets of the Greeks: he did it in the plays of Aristophanes, and in the treatises of Theophrastus. He portrayed the Greeks' public and private lives. Aristophanes and Theophrastus did for the Greeks what Molière alone did for the French. It would be a great honor for two people to do what Molière did on his own.

Once there was nothing more to add about the weaknesses and absurdities of Athens, Asmodeus was called Terence, and this time around he dabbled in Roman comedy, with little success. At the time, Rome was too similar to Athens to furnish fresh material for comedy. Rome was then just like us today: always busy, always bustling, pleasure-seeking, vain, lacking self-doubt, moderately nice and moderately mean, but always moderately mediocre, as far from freedom as from slavery; skeptical out of fatigue, jaded, bored, waiting for things to come to an end, having been through the heights of human glory, and now disabused of glory. In a word, people without passion, without beliefs, without misfortune, without hope, and without virtue. Thus comedy passed over Rome without stopping. It found Roman manners too unassuming to linger there for too long. Comedy skidded on those manners as on a polished surface. Later on, when there were all sorts of disruptions, such as when an emperor appointed his horse first consul,[12] and his male friend an empress, Comedy backed away in horror. And so Comedy became satire. Asmodeus had to escape as fast as his legs would carry him when he found himself forced to be called Juvenal.[13]

Comedy and the portrayal of manners require the following: people who are original; an era that is well-established but that still has some life left in it; a particular character, activity, vigor, and strength of spirit, soul, and body. Times of decline are not propitious for a writer whose job is to describe and observe.

So, Asmodeus, why don't you take leave of aging Greece and Rome and move on to the Middle Ages and join some bawdy priest who knows the price of a bottle? Give up the philosopher's beard, break the cynic's barrel, sell the Roman knight's gold ring to buy some booze, become a monk, go to Rome, see the Holy Father, then come back to France and go look at the king. Throw yourself headlong into the world of heresies, of pious men, of army men, of clergy, of courtiers. Be there for the awakening of the French spirit in France and the ver-

---

[12] The Roman emperor Caligula was rumored to have planned to appoint his horse, Incitatus, as consul. Here Janin also refers to Caligula's alleged same-sex partners. These and other stories were presented by contemporary commentators as signs of Caligula's insanity, but they have not been corroborated by reliable sources.

[13] A Roman poet, author of the collection *The Satires* in the early second century.

nacular in Italy. Make equal fun of the victors and the vanquished, of the holy fathers standing up and those who are kneeling at altars. Make fun of the king and the courtiers, of the scholar and the layperson. Speak about vice, good grub, girls of easy virtue at the tavern's door. Speak about everything and in all languages: in French, in Latin, in Spanish. Above all, speak in your incisive French language, gentle Asmodeus, and after that, accept France's sincere gratitude, because you gave France her language and her first great book, *Pantagruel*.[14] Later on, you will give France La Fontaine[15] and Molière. Let us all bow down before Asmodeus in Rabelais's clothes!

In the seventeenth century, Asmodeus shed his monk's garb. He then dressed as a bourgeois. He turned his life around. He became a modest dinner companion in a household of a wealthy aristocratic patron. He learned Greek for the third time! He busied himself with grammar. He grappled with a learned, elegant, and exact phrasing that had all the freedom of the style of antiquity. Asmodeus was now modestly called La Bruyère. He painted the customs of his time with all the taste

---

[14] A classic of the French Renaissance, the 1532 satirical novel by François Rabelais features scatological humor and exalts bodily pleasures.
[15] Jean de La Fontaine was a French writer particularly well known for his fables.

and grace of a writer of yesteryear. He concerned himself with the slightest of social nuances, with the most fragile of flaws, with the most innocent of oddities. He lived on crumbs that fell off the table belonging to the Misanthrope and Tartuffe.[16] He was excellent, exquisite, good company, and of impeccable taste, and, it should be mentioned, he displayed these qualities for the first time since his departure from Greece.

Then, one day, while the seventeenth century continued to shine its light on France—a country that was leaning toward philosophy and civil and religious liberty instead of poetry—the demon of observation became known as Voltaire: an insatiable joker, intrepid misanthrope, a man who laughs at the penitents, a man who brands humanity with a hot iron in the middle of its forehead! These were exhausting times for our devil. He was not used to being sober and mean. He had been the critic of his own nature. He had been happily engaged in a double libertinage of style and manners. He had been comical and jovial; he bit but he did not hurt! He raged, but no hard feelings. He had been Rabelais and not Voltaire; he became Voltaire and wrote *Candide*. He backed away from *Candide* as he had backed away from the satires of Juvenal, and, to comfort himself, he wrote *The*

---

[16] *Le misanthrope* (1666) and *Tartuffe* (1664) are plays by Molière.

Marriage of Figaro.[17] *Figaro* is Asmodeus at the height of
his wit and audacity. It's Asmodeus at his most mischievous, a young Asmodeus, brilliant and giddy, who floats
in the air, who bursts out laughing, makes his fortune,
and later on will become a good bourgeois.

But alas! Asmodeus didn't have time to be a bourgeois.
He spent his mature years in a magician's bottle. He aged
in that bottle, and came out thanks to a student's whim.
This is when we saw him hunched and limping, hobbling
slowly with a walking stick as a punishment. As I said
before, these were good times for sketching manners.
Asmodeus would remove the roofs of houses and expose men lying in their beds and women before they got
dressed. In those days, Asmodeus behaved decently, unlike the way he would behave later on. Eventually, he got
a ragpicker's sack. He looked for stories in all the sewers
of Paris. Not long before that, he was on top of shining
roofs; we saw him out and about, a lantern in hand; a
misshapen hook replaced his elegant walking stick.
Previously, he wrote his books on the back of Fiction,
a young prostitute with perfumed hair who would lend
him her white shoulder, half-crouching, and give him
an understanding smile. But now he is very different.

---

[17] *The Marriage of Figaro* (1778) is a play by Beaumarchais. Spirited and
irreverent, the character of Figaro is associated with resisting abuse of
power by the aristocracy.

Nowadays he is the one crouching by a border stone while writing his tablets. Asmodeus! A true demon! A spiritual madman! A bottomless critic! He managed to find charming objects even in his ragpicker's sack! He managed to write masterpieces even while writing on a stone! Alas! Yet again, these were good times for writing. Power was displaced and the royal court took flight! This time around, it wasn't the aristocrats who were ridiculous or immoral. It was the people who were ridiculous and immoral, for they took the king's place.

But today, having used all sorts of disguises, having become a *hermit*, like all old devils, what will Asmodeus say?[18] What sort of portrait could he make of our bland manners? Today, the old world of comedy has disappeared like those islands in the ocean devoured by a volcano that drift toward the unknown continents. Today, we no longer find any of the old comic types. Today, no more greedy fathers, no more gullible wives, no more wayward and gambling children, no more handsome

---

[18] *L'hermite de la Chaussée d'Antin* (*The Hermit of the Chaussée d'Antin*) was a column written by Victor-Joseph Étienne under the name Étienne de Jouy and published in *La gazette de France* (*The Gazette of France*) from 1811 to 1814. This work is also considered a precursor of the *physiologies* and other works of urban observation published in the 1830s and 1840s. The *hermite* of the title traveled through different parts of Paris and reported his observations of different aspects of urban life.

Leandres[19] who congratulate themselves on not paying their debts, no more manservants who become their master's companions in debauchery.[20] Today, adultery is hidden out of sheer embarrassment, debts are considered shameful, gambling habits are concealed. People believe in God out of self-respect, they don't ruin themselves out of respect for others. Today, the high-society lady is affable and good, rather than absurd like Madame d'Escarbagnas;[21] mothers are educated without being pedantic;[22] young girls are innocent but don't ask naive questions like Agnès.[23] Today, the miser's son greets his father with respect when he meets him in the street. Bartholo's ward avoids befriending her guardian's barber.[24] Today, Diafoirus doesn't have a medical practice and Purgon is everyone's laughing stock, and should we meet Molière's imaginary invalid on our way, we would offer him our arm and inquire with interest, "How are

---

[19] A character in Molière's comedy *Les fourberies de Scapin* (1671; *Scapin the Schemer*).

[20] A reference to *The Barber of Seville* (1773), by Beaumarchais.

[21] A reference to *La comtesse d'Escarbagnas* (1671; *The Countess of Escarbagnas*), a one-act comedy by Molière.

[22] A reference to *Les femmes savantes* (1672; *The Learned Ladies*), a comedy by Molière.

[23] A central character in Molière's *École des femmes* (1663; *The School for Wives*) known for her extreme naïveté about worldly matters.

[24] A reference to *The Barber of Seville*.

you feeling?"[25] Today, we would negotiate the Misanthrope's promissory notes at the stock exchange, send
all of Regnard's manservants to the galleys,[26] and send
the judge to the Bicêtre mental asylum for ten years. Madame George Dandin would be locked up in an asylum
for former prostitutes for the rest of her days, and her
brother would spend six months in jail.[27] Today, Cheru-
bin would be in school and given bread and water for
causing mischief.[28] Today, we would not put up with all
those poets' whims, with all the exasperating dramas,
with all those furious relationships—we haven't believed
in any of this for a long while. We are sensible, serious,
and honest people; we have overcome ridicule; we are
all, so to speak, the bourgeois gentleman who made the
most of our lessons in orthography, philosophy, dance,
and even fencing![29] Woe to those rhyme-makers! No
longer could a man of wit who wanted to make fun of

---

[25] Diafoirus and Purgon are medical quacks in *Le malade imaginaire*
(1673; *The Imaginary Invalid*).
[26] Jean-François Regnard was a seventeenth-century French playwright and author of comedies. He is considered one of Molière's most
accomplished successors.
[27] *George Dandin* (1668) is a play by Molière. In Janin's France, some
former prostitutes lived out their lives in penitential, convent-like
homes, where their hair was cut off and they wore clothing made of
rough homespun fabric.
[28] A character in *The Marriage of Figaro*.
[29] A reference to Molière's comedy *Le bourgeois gentilhomme* (1670; *The
Bourgeois Gentleman*).

France do so simply by virtue of being witty. No longer could the most sacred things be subject to ridicule: husbands, debtors, innocent young girls, mothers and fathers, respect for elders, respect for the law, respect for the fatherland, all those things that old comedy so wickedly abused. All of us were complicit in this. We dared laugh at such cruel buffoonery. Today, this buffoonery is outdated. We no longer laugh at it; the times of such cruel jokes have passed. We marry, we love our wives, our children respect us, we respect the moneylenders more than anyone else, we pay our debts right away or else are sent to the Saint-Pélagie prison. As for publicly mocking virtue, this is another thing that went out of fashion. Nobody tolerates this sort of thing any longer, not even some marquis.

So, dear reader, do wake up Asmodeus today if you wish, shake him out of his inaction, make him act and speak. But there is no knowing what his words or actions will be. Once again, where are you, Asmodeus? Which enchanter has you still? In which glass prison are you still hiding? Break all the fragrance flasks, open ladies' most precious perfume bottles, call loudly upon Asmodeus! Asmodeus will not respond. Asmodeus is nowhere to be found. That's because Asmodeus is everywhere. Asmodeus is no one in particular. Asmodeus is everyone. No one in particular is a joker these days. By contrast, everyone studies manners and corrects others: buffoons and critics abound. It is through this revolution in the study of manners that this new limping devil will redeem himself, if at all possible. It is by means of collaboration among all people that he will once again write the ever-changing story of all our quirks. Be kind to him, please! Recognize him in this new form. You knew him in the form of analysis, elegant and jovial. Recognize him now in the form of serious, decent, and reverential synthesis. We are entering once again into a new way of portraying manners. Unable to produce comedy with just one man, we now do so with more than a hundred.[30] What does it matter if it's a hundred or just two? It's the same for unity. If unity is lost, interest will be gained. Even if we lose Asmodeus, we still gain famous figures who will come dressed in his coat but without his stick, to reveal to contemporaries what they have seen, what they have heard, what they have learned about our modern civilization: a civilization so uneven, so varied, so wavering that its most innocent whim became a revolution.

---

[30] A reference to the collection of vignettes by 101 writers to which this text serves as introduction.

The Gamin of Paris

From *Paris; or,*
The Book of a Hundred and One

The gamin de Paris, or Paris street urchin, is one of the central archetypes in the nineteenth-century French cultural imagination. A working-class boy, this figure appears most prominently in Eugène Delacroix's 1830 painting La Liberté guidant le peuple *(Liberty Leading the People), which features a youth in tattered clothes and a schoolboy's beret on top of a barricade, brandishing a pistol alongside the allegorical, bare-breasted Lady Liberty. The gamin is then most fully fleshed out in Victor Hugo's monumental 1862 novel* Les Misérables, *through the character of Gavroche.*

During the years of the July Monarchy (1830–1848), the figure of the gamin appeared in numerous works of popular literature, including an 1836 vaudeville by Jean-François Bayard and Émile Vanderbuch; "Le Gamin de Paris," by Jules Janin, from Les Français peints par eux-mêmes: Encyclopédie morale du dix-neuvième siècle *(The French Depicted by Themselves: A Moral Encyclopedia of the Nineteenth Century); and* Physiologie du gamin de Paris, galopin industriel *(1842; Physiology of the Gamin of Paris, a Thieving Rascal), by Ernest Bourget, as well as the essay below. As is the case with other social types of this period, the gamin shares many of his defining features across different texts and yet is not monolithic—for example, d'Outrepont's gamin is much more ideologically inflected than the one we find in Janin's text.*[1]

---

[1] For an extensive discussion of the figure of the gamin, see Brown.

Naples has its lazzaroni; Venice, its condottieri;[2] every town in France has residents who are unusual. But we Parisians have nothing to be jealous about, for we have our gamin!

To write the history of Paris without first talking about the gamin! . . . You might as well begin the history of Rome with Brutus without mentioning the kings who founded it. It's like pretending that a population is just there, without giving an account of where it came from.

The gamin, whose name is impossible to translate into any language, is a child of the city. The streets are his cradle; they witness his first smile and his first steps. An obedient son, he does not leave his mother's bosom. You can find him on every corner, in every form, in every trade.

Like the gods of India, like the Holy Ampulla,[3] like the pagan gods, like the milk of the Virgin, like the Dalai Lama, like thousands of other divinities whose sa-

---

[2] Lazzaroni were homeless beggars from the city of Naples. The word (spelled *lazaroni* in the original text) derives from the Hospital of St. Lazarus, which often served as a shelter for these individuals. Condottieri were mercenaries hired by the Italian city-states, such as Venice.

[3] A glass vial that held the anointing oil for the coronation of the kings of France.

cred nature we can't deny, the gamin is immortal! He always stays young. Since the foundation of Paris, he has been pounding the pavement. Wait a minute . . . the pavement? The gamin existed long before Paris had pavement. He splashed around in mud in the eleventh century. I daresay he witnessed the first kings, and he knows better than any historian, even members of the Academy, who King Pharamond was.[4]

If Paris had existed in the time of Julius Caesar, the gamin would no doubt have escorted his chariot; because by his very nature he is part of all the triumphs, all the celebrations, just like the city authorities, the people of the *juste milieu*,[5] the food distributors, and the police officers.

He is part of every mourning ritual, along with the funeral home workers and the authorities, except he is not wearing crepe.[6] He attends the funerals of members of all political parties. He remains neutral, which is the right thing to do. He takes advantage of victories without worrying about consequences. He drinks the wine of

---

[4] A legendary early king of the Franks.

[5] Literally "happy medium," this term was used to describe the policies of the July Monarchy, which initially strove to achieve political moderation.

[6] Heavy silk fabric often used for mourning attire.

the victor, just as he would have drunk that of the vanquished, if the latter had been in the mood to pay for it.

He pounces upon dried sausage without any fear of humiliation—and you thought he wasn't philosophical!

He loves public festivities, because good manners do not preclude him from enjoying them. Then, he is entitled to the sticks after the fireworks are over. He exclaims, "Long live everyone!" "Down with everyone!" And he is not paid by anyone to do that. He does it for his own pleasure, out of idleness, for no reason. As long as there is noise, he doesn't care. What's the risk? Sure, it would be nice to keep order, but he is a child, free and wearing rags. He is not worried about losing his shoes in the crowd. He often doesn't even have any shoes. He joyfully throws himself into anything that brings about movement and revels in it. He is happy when he can destroy something . . . Ah! Lucky him, he doesn't own anything. How many of those who shout from the tribune would have done the same, if they had not been required to own property to become a deputy?

The gamin himself represents the intimate character of man—not those men we see trapped on theater balconies, their hands bound in leather gloves so white and so fine that you can't help admiring them for their mechanical perfection. Rather, I mean a man who is calm and fervent, furious and detached, with all his passions exposed, as if Asmodeus did to the man's heart what he did to Madrid's roofs.[7]

The gamin is made of the same stuff as a man. He is and is not a lot of things. He is a man and a child; he is all and he is nothing; he is courageous and cowardly, brave and faint-hearted; he is proud like a man; he crawls like an upstart courtier. One moment he is serious; the next he is laughing his head off like a happy child. He could be a joker, playing nasty tricks like Punch and Judy at the fair. He is witty like a child of Paris, or dumb, yes, dumb, but with that stupidity of the peasants that exposes the affected shrewdness of the city dweller.

The gamin is compassionate. He will do you a favor if he feels like it, and if he has nothing better to do. He will be cruel if it brings him pleasure. He will take pity on a poor devil who gets hurt in the street, and moments later you will see him pull a ladder that, when it falls, will surely kill the worker perched on top. The evil deed done, he will run away, because he is aware of his weakness and cherishes impunity above all. He is not the only one who has run away like that or will do so in the future.

---

[7] The demon Asmodeus is a character in the popular 1707 novel *Le diable boiteux* (*The Devil upon Two Sticks*), by Alain-René Lesage. Lesage's demon explores the city of Madrid and the everyday life of its inhabitants by removing rooftops and peeking inside people's homes. See "Asmodeus," the essay by Janin in this volume.

Other times, carefree like Diogenes,[8] he plays in the streets. If he is coming home late and is afraid of being beaten, there is nothing to fear. He has the best recipe for avoiding punishment: he simply doesn't come home. He cares not for rain or wind; he cares not if he ruins his clothes. He is at home in the streets. The streets belong to him.

You own a house. Very well, but the boundaries of the house belong to the gamin more than to you. There he is, getting settled there to play; try chasing him away and he will make fun of you. If you try to use physical force, he will go away. But what's a few blows to him? He always comes out on top and will come back to mock you. Some homeowners take offense at this.

Before going any further, it would be good, I think, to paint a portrait of our hero.

The gamin is between ten and fifteen years old. Son of a worker, he is an apprentice. When you meet him, he will likely be running errands for the bourgeois, the master, or the boss. Perhaps even, since education is everywhere these days, he will be going to his neighborhood's mutual school.[9] In the early days, he was enrolled at the

---

[8] A Greek philosopher and one of the founders of Cynicism.
[9] Mutual school was a method of teaching popularized in the late eighteenth and early nineteenth centuries: a form of active and coop-

school run by the Christian Brothers.[10] You should have seen him play practical jokes on the brothers! You've been to school, right? So you can easily imagine what children who don't fear a punishment of dry bread and water are capable of. That's the only thing the gamin eats anyway. You can't take away his outings. As for the punishment of writing sentences, you're out of luck: he doesn't know how to write. The only way to punish him is to hurt his self-esteem: make him wear a dunce cap or donkey ears. But, frankly, he takes it in stride. Nobody ever died of that anyway. You want to beat him up? He will defend himself. Judge for yourself.

You will find the gamin working for shoemakers, carpenters, locksmiths, house painters, printers, and wallpaper installers. He might be nothing on his own, but he is everything thanks to his insolence.

The gamin does not have a particular attire. Sometimes he might wear a green apron or a shirt blackened by iron; sometimes, a paper bonnet, a meager cap, a Greek-style skullcap. As for stockings, that's a luxury; no handkerchief either. What is it for, anyway? His tattered

erative learning in which one teacher was charged with all administrative functions.

[10] The Frères Ignorantins, or Frères des Écoles Chrétiennes, were a religious fraternity founded in the seventeenth century for the purpose of providing free education to the children of the poor. The brothers were required to give their services without charge.

shirt peeks through his ripped pants and completes his outfit. The gamin must have ripped clothing, or, at the very least, he should wear mismatched items. It's impossible not to have fun when you have all this freedom. The gamin plays constantly. For him life is just pure pleasure until the age of fifteen. What a difference between his childhood, so full, so varied, so beautiful, and the one led by your children, my dear reader. Instead of being dressed to the nines in the morning, the gamin is free to do as he pleases. He does not have some tyrant hovering over him each minute of the day, telling him at every turn, "Monsieur will get dirty!" "Monsieur plays in the sand!" "Monsieur will rip his pants!" Monsieur wanted to climb on a bench and now he is walking away crying. "What a naughty child!" exclaim the nannies whose conversation he has interrupted. "He will come home all dirty! Gracious! How naughty!" and the child starts crying again. It's all your fault. Why do you confine him when all he wants to do is spread his wings?* I bet if you

* This reminds me of a little anecdote that I think is very appropriate here. The first day of the year 1806, the mother of the young prince Louis of Holland (adopted heir to the throne of Napoleon)—a princess who was so ingenious that she made herself loved by all who surrounded her and who was truly so good and so attentive, so full of concern for her son—promised to give him as a New Year's gift all that he asked for. "Oh, please, Mommy dearest," responded the child when he saw the Amsterdam gardens soaked from the previous night's rain, "Oh, please let me play a little bit in the mud!" [Note in original text.]

told your child, if he is at least three years old, that he had to wear tattered clothes, he'd get upset. That's also your fault. Your greed instilled pride in him. That's because if this poor little kid rips his flimsy jacket while playing soldiers, you will scold him, you will get madder at him than at a grown-up, and for good reason. A child doesn't understand your reasons for such fury, but I know it all too well. You will have to buy him new clothes, and your pride will clash with your wallet. But my gamin, if once in his lifetime by some miracle he finds a new outfit in the folds of his dad's old redingote,[11] and if it gets ripped, he is told, "You will wear it ripped." So be it, he will wear it ripped. He doesn't care because he always wears rags. It's his condition, his future for months to come. Why would he ever miss out on the fun just to keep poverty at bay for a bit? Why would he not climb a tree on the boulevard for such a trifle? Oh, no, he will surely go for it. What will he get out of it? He will have the advantage of seeing his reflection in the café windows where he is not allowed to enter; so it's well worth it! The gamin is far too philosophical to sacrifice a moment of happiness to vanity. He plays in the streets. His clothing does not grant him access to your promenades. And what would

---

[11] The man's redingote was a double-breasted outer garment, popular in the late eighteenth and early nineteenth centuries.

he do there anyway? Nothing! He needs his peers. It's with them that he breathes freely. This is where he belongs! Yet he was not always a stranger to your sunny gardens. When the people ruled, the gamin enjoyed the same privileges as a royal child.

You who are reading this right now, you are at the very least a taxpayer and a warrant officer of the national guard.[12] So you are too highly placed in this world even to cast your eyes upon a poor child. But do look at those who are still governed by nature, despite your best efforts. Your own children have in them a spirit of freedom that does not deceive them. This precious freedom that you take away from them, they sense it in the children of the people. When the gamin passes by your own son, your aristocratic flesh and blood turns around with envy. I have seen so many of these poor victims as they obediently march around the Tuileries garden, flanked by a big servant all decked out, busy speaking drivel to the young maid, so blonde and fresh, and so much prettier than his mistress! If Monsieur manages the house, or even sometimes when it's Madame, a brilliant gentleman

---

[12] The warrant officer, or sergeant-major, holds the top noncommissioned rank. The character described here—a taxpayer (who has enough money to pay taxes but is not quite middle-class) and a warrant officer—is mocked here for having middle-class pretensions. Although only at the edge of the middle class, he thinks too highly of himself to notice the gamin.

parades his panache before the presumptive heir to the peerage, a shaky institution these days.[13] How many of these budding notables have I seen being dragged along while their gaze is longingly fixed on the gamin, who, looking happy, a flower in his mouth, his worker's apron slightly pulled up, is singing at the top of his lungs a tune he recently heard playing on the barrel organ! He looks so free and easy, my gamin, next to your mechanical doll of a child! He carries with him the air of freedom that a child from a good home cannot help but see, because he sighs at the sight of someone happier than himself! He senses his own inferiority and aches to receive a smile from the plebeian. Right away he is discouraged from pursuing his desire: "Come here, monsieur, and leave that little rascal alone." "Little rascal" is the name given to children of the working classes! That's how you educate your children, by instilling in them disdain for the people. Just you wait, your turn will come.

Enough about you, children of high society. Go ahead and remain under the watch of an army of servants. As for me, I will return to my favorite child, the child of

---

[13] Peerage is a hereditary distinction within French nobility dating back to the Middle Ages. The title of peer was an extraordinary honor bestowed on a very small number of people. During the Restoration (1814–1830), the Chamber of Peers was granted a constitutional function. The institution of peerage was abolished in 1848.

Paris, the gamin, whom I love because he is himself, because by loving him I know exactly whom I love. In him I see the origins of free and strong men.

There is no school for the gamin. He won't waste his childhood sitting around the classroom. He is better than that—he lives. With one hour a day of studying at most, he won't become a pedant, but he will learn just enough to read our unequal laws and to understand them when they concern him. What more does he need? Do you bother yourself with regulations that restrict small businesses? Above all, he will know enough to recognize the signal from his father's rifle.

I like to observe the gamin in his natural habitat. It's a way to study human nature. But to do so, you will need to go find him, because, just like great nobilities, the gamin doesn't bother seeking anyone out. Too bad for you if, when you wish to make his acquaintance, you're too lazy to find him on his own turf. Too bad for you, you won't see him, and if you don't see him, it will be your loss.

Every neighborhood in Paris gives birth to a gamin. He belongs to the whole city. Still, there are some parts that he is particularly fond of. If you want to study him, go to the Boulevard du Temple, where he appears in all his different forms. He struts, he comes and goes, with nothing to do or worry about, like a true gamin: nose in the air, with a mocking look and a brave demeanor. He has just spent an hour watching a magician, and now he will kill some time at a parade. Idleness is his essence, but an Italian-style idleness, one he savors. You will see him there, devoted entirely to his street-urchin lifestyle, as he bumps into everyone and doesn't even mind when he is pushed away. He knows he is not the strongest, and his honor is not compromised for such a trifle. So many have received blows, including those of public opinion, and they keep on marching with their head held high. Besides, the gamin will fight you. You've invaded his sanctuary, so he will pull on your coat, he will tease your dog. Woe to you if you're wearing tailcoats! You will respond by hitting him with your cane, and this is the only way you will have the upper hand. What am I saying? He is undeterred even by that. That which has just angered you, he turns against someone else, or maybe he will attack you from many sides, all the while laughing and jumping around. Oh, what a beautiful life!

You have a carriage, and he has one as well! He climbs in the back of coaches and cabriolets,[14] he clings to the back, and yet is not a footman. His fellow gamin passing by yells to the driver, "Driver, hit the kid in the back!" Oh, well, he gets off and waits for the next carriage. How

---

[14] The cabriolet is a two-wheeled carriage with a folding hood, pulled by one horse.

can you be mad at him even when he is teasing you, when he is so joyful you would think he was born under the sunny skies of Italy on the day of carnival. He has no sorrows, no future, everything is in the present for him, and the present is beautiful when you're twelve years old and have not been stuck in school. He saunters around with such abandon; his life is all joy, all pleasure; it's a life of Harlequin—Harlequin from Bergamo, with his bat and a rabbit tail. It's a life of Harlequin when he was little and not in love, with the reason of Polichinelle and the foolishness of our own Jeannot.[15] It's a truism that bears repeating: his silly jokes work all the time because in them you always recognize someone you know.

The gamin loves to gamble, he is crazy for it. Didn't I tell you that he has all the traits of a grown man? He gambles away his pennies with passion. You, on the other hand, gamble with gold; that's a big difference. The gamin's national game, his most favorite one, is the game of corks.[16] You have to have a good eye and dexterity, not like in your games . . . oh, pardon me, I forgot that these days you need great skill to win a game of whist.

------

[15] Polichinelle, Jeannot, and Arlequin are stock characters from the Italian commedia dell'arte who appeared in French popular theater. Arlequin wore a characteristic checkered costume and is thought to have originated in the Italian city of Bergamo.

[16] The French equivalent of the game of spoons, known as *jeu de bouchon*, is played with corks.

The gamin gambles with all he has, sometimes even with what he doesn't have. He borrows, then pays or doesn't pay when he loses. But all the winnings stay within the gamin brotherhood, so no harm, no foul! Besides, since the time of Figaro,[17] many others haven't paid what they owed or fulfilled their commitments. The gallery applauds when a cork is turned over by a brave blow. If there are any disputes, a spectator's cane intervenes, and the winner can stack his coins in a tall pile. The gamin never refuses a rematch, but once the loser admits defeat, the winnings are converted into chestnuts, fruit, and potato fries, and everyone is invited to enjoy the treat. What can you do? You can't possibly go to the Cadran-Bleu[18] with just a few coins.

And if a fight arises, no need to walk around sour-faced for hours. Jackets and caps come off right away, kicks and punches rain down from all directions, and afterwards, everyone is friends again. Nobody fires a blank, nobody dines at Gillet's; but the fight was honest. Civilized fights are too refined.

The gamin possesses a sense of justice that would do honor to a war council or a court, even one presided over

---

[17] The protagonist of Beaumarchais's *Le barbier de Seville* (*The Barber of Seville*) and *Le mariage de Figaro* (*The Marriage of Figaro*).

[18] A restaurant dating to the pre-Revolutionary era known as a gathering place for playwrights.

by a lawyer at the royal court. If he sees another gamin about to be defeated by a bigger one, he will join the weaker one to recalibrate the balance. He will go into battle without a care, without fear, without reason, solely out of the goodness of his heart and out of principle. Isn't that what modern politics is all about?

Just like you, the gamin has his favorite shows. The Boulevard du Temple is full of theaters where hilarity reigns, where you can laugh out loud,[19] where you can even think out loud. Everyone is free because everyone can shut up those who bother them. There, the gamin is in his element. Like a journalist or an author, the gamin rarely pays for his ticket. Thanks to his cunning nature, he always manages to get in for free. A tireless self-advocate, he implores the passersby, "Oh, my dear bourgeois, I only need two pennies to go see a show, please give me two pennies, my dear bourgeois!" If you refuse him his two pennies, he sticks his tongue out at you, makes faces, and runs off to pester someone else. Chances are that this trick, repeated a good two dozen times, earns him the twelve pennies he needs for a ticket.

---

[19] The Boulevard du Temple was famous for numerous popular theaters, including the Théâtre de la Gaîté, the Théâtre des Funambules, the Théâtre Lyrique, and the Théâtre des Folies-Dramatiques, among others. At one point the boulevard was nicknamed the Boulevard du Crime because of the many melodramas played in its theaters.

And so there he goes, our gamin, to the ticket counter in the foyer, talking loudly and pushing everyone out of the way. He pushes so that he can get to the front and make himself comfortable. If he is hot, he takes his jacket off; if he is bored, he just relies on one of his other qualities: those of a speculator. He's off again, reselling his ticket. He is so much more fortunate than you, who are obliged to rent an expensive theater box so that you can see a bad play with bad actors. He has his place reserved and nobody can touch it. It's like the royal box in our elite theaters, except the one belonging to this king of the boulevards is always full. The gamin fills it to capacity with his popular vigor. His plays are good and his actors are good. He doesn't yawn at the ridiculous romantic dramas. He does not fall asleep at the classic-soporific tragedies, but he laughs his head off at a pantomime that evokes the infancy of art, where the unfortunate Pierrot Desbureaux,[20] the best mime of a period already so rich in mimes, is tormented by the Harlequin and his old jokes. The gamin laughs so hard at such frank depictions of this honest servant's tribulations: he never succeeds at anything and is hoodwinked by a swindler throughout the entire play. The gamin laughs, and the people laugh

---

[20] Jean-Gaspard Deburau (misspelled in the original) was a French-Bohemian mime who popularized the role of Pierrot, a sad mime and a stock character of the commedia dell'arte.

too, because they experience scenes like this every day. They are such great philosophers.

The nosebleed section suits the gamin best. It's the least expensive one. He struts in there, eats nuts, and throws the shells into the orchestra seats. He gets a coco drink[21] from the seller but spills half his glass on the balcony below. Then he bursts into peals of laughter at the bad mood of those he has baptized with this licorice-flavored juice.

During intermission, the gamin climbs the iron gate and performs Madame Saqui's famous feat[22] the way you yourself hum the famous diva Cinti's cavatine when you come out of the opera. Freedom offers so many pleasures!

The gamin scoffs at a police officer as he snatches a lantern in order to confuse a coachman's horses. So what if he is caught red-handed attaching the chestnut vendor's cart to the wheel of a carriage? How could he possibly pay the fine? His clothes are worth nothing. A few blows, and that's that, and everyone laughs as much at his misadventures as at those of the poor vendor, who is picking his chestnuts out of the gutter to finish roasting them.

-----

[21] A popular drink made of water and licorice.
[22] Marguerite-Antoinette Lalanne, or Madame Saqui, was a famous tightrope walker.

The gamin will slip between your legs into the crowd. Maybe he will even pinch you, but good luck catching him. The crowds, the throngs of people, are his element. Because he is naughty, he goes wherever there is mischief to be done. He goes wherever there is fun to be had, because he is a child. As I was just saying, he loves noise, just for the sake of making noise. As long as the gamin has existed, and by consequence, as long as Paris has existed, he has been involved in every single riot, in every single disturbance. He stands on the sidelines of the revolt, not fearing bullets whistling by. During the times of the Catholic League, he would follow alongside the processions singing, and then all of a sudden would scream, "Long live the king of Navarre!"[23] A blow with a flat side of the sword would shut him up. A man would have been killed, but not him, a child! He was not important. No one would dare hurt him. He was the only one in France who fully enjoyed inviolability.

Before that era, he was there on Saint Bartholomew's Day when, on the night of August 23, the Louvre's big

---

[23] The Catholic League played a major role in the French Wars of Religion in the sixteenth century. It was first organized in 1576 under the leadership of Henri, duc de Guise (also known as Henri I de Lorraine), to defend the Catholic religion against the Protestant Reformation and to oppose concessions granted to the Protestants by the French king. The League was involved in an unsuccessful attempt to prevent Henri de Navarre (later Henri IV of France) from inheriting the French throne.

bell gave the signal to start the massacre.[24] The gamin was the first out there in the streets as though he had been in on the conspiracy. He walked with a firm step, curious to see what was going on. And you know exactly what he saw!

He lived through all the bloody moments of history with a clear conscience. He was not armed but could have attacked a defenseless man (as did so many others). He saw suffering without causing it, just to educate himself, and educate himself he did.

During our great Revolution, the gamin followed the combatants. During the Reign of Terror, he followed the carts transporting those condemned to the guillotine. He did so not out of anger but out of idleness. What did he have to lose? He who is always free was surely unafraid of being locked up in the Bastille, and yet he was there during the storming of the Bastille. He entered without any weapons. He nailed shut a cannon, not for security but because it was fun, because it's always amus-

---

[24] The Saint Bartholomew's Day massacre was a wave of assassinations and mob killings of French Protestants (Huguenots) by the Catholics during the French Wars of Religion. The massacre followed the wedding of Marguerite de Valois, the French king's sister, to Henri de Navarre (the future Henri IV of France). Many of the Huguenot leaders and luminaries who had gathered in Paris for the royal wedding were killed. The massacre was one of the bloodiest episodes of civil violence in French history.

ing to be able to yell, "Hey, you, Chauvin, I just nailed a cannon shut!"[25] He would have done the same with the revolutionaries' weapons if he had gotten the chance. And yet, when medals were awarded, he didn't get a single one, not even a July Cross.[26] Unlike the gamin, so many people wear this medal even though they were not there.

It was during those hot July days that I became convinced more than ever of the gamin's great importance to the state. I saw him build the barricades; I saw him yank stones out of the pavement and bring them into houses to throw at the royal troupes. He too did his part for liberty! On top of a roof, his feet dangling over the Porte Saint-Denis, he threw stones while yelling, "Long live the Charter!"[27] Poor kid!

I saw him all alone, like a true Don Quixote, advancing with a stick in his hand, against an entire squadron! He could pillage any weapon, but he took none because he didn't like any of them. He plundered an archdiocese

---

[25] Nicolas Chauvin was an apocryphal figure of a French revolutionary soldier distinguished by his excessive devotion to the revolutionary army and then to the Napoleonic army.

[26] The July Cross, created by King Louis-Philippe d'Orleans on 13 December 1831, was awarded to those who demonstrated courage during the July Revolution of 1830, which overthrew the Restoration monarchy and marked the end of the Bourbon dynasty.

[27] "Vive la Charte!" ("Long live the Charter!") was a rallying cry of the people during the July Revolution.

to destroy it, not to keep anything for himself. By contrast, those who are paid to preserve end up destroying for their own profit.

Finally, to conclude his great deeds, he got wounded on the Place Vendôme. The last artillery discharge cost him a runny nose. Every time you see him, he appears to be mocking you with his long, disheveled hair; his turned-up nose and his sardonic smile; his jeering and insolent looks. It's his way of being. It's too bad if you don't like it; others like it just fine. The gamin! He is Charlet's adopted son![28] Charlet has immortalized him with his pencil. He will show the gamin to you in a thousand different ways, like a lover who paints his mistress. Look, do you see him over there, with his big book, his eyes, his good-heartedness, his naively profound reflections? The gamin, along with an old soldier, is the subject of choice of our national painter. And the choice of these two heroes was very thoughtful. The portrait shows the people in infancy and in an age of decline. The two extremes come together.

If you ask Charlet what became of the gamin, he will point out the old soldier. The cheerfulness of a repub-

---

[28] Nicolas Toussaint Charlet was a French designer and painter especially known for depicting military themes and subjects.

lican gamin can be found once again in the drunken stance of an invalid decorated at Marengo.[29]

And if you want to know something else, you will learn that the gamin of 1815, the one who greeted the aristocrats coming back from exile[30] in true gamin fashion, has grown up. You will also learn that he returned to the Louvre, a rifle covered with black powder in hand, and respected national property. He only took a few shots, and then he drank the king's wine. It was yet more child's play. If you ask me once more what will become of that kid who just the other day was playing with the cartridge pouches of the Royal Guard killed on the Place du Palais-Royal, I will tell you, if in a few years you become a minister and decide to imitate your predecessors, you'd better watch out. My gamin of today will be a grown man. He will grab the rifle his father carried yesterday and his arm will have gained the strength needed to raise it. So, Monsieur Minister, you who might dabble in despotism, your chest will become his target, and I would be careful if I were you. He has good aim.

---

[29] The Battle of Marengo (14 June 1800) was fought between the Napoleon-led French army and the Austrians, in Piedmont, Italy.

[30] Many members of the aristocracy, exiled during the revolution, returned to France at the advent of the Bourbon Restoration.

EUGÉNIE FOA

The Fashionable Woman and the Elegant Woman in 1833

From *Paris; or, The Book of a Hundred and One*

Eugénie Foa (née Rebecca Eugénie Rodrigues Henriquès) was likely the first Jewish author to publish fiction in French. Born into a prominent Sephardic family, Foa turned to writing in order to support herself and her two children after she was abandoned by her husband. She published several novels and short stories, frequently contributed to the contemporary press, and was particularly well known for her children's books. She also wrote for Les voix des femmes *(Women's Voices), a feminist journal (see Leff).*

"So last year"

I say in 1833, because, as you can imagine, a fashionable woman in 1833 is not at all the same as one in 1832, and will most certainly be different from one in 1834. Alas! Her reign often does not even last that long. I've known some women whose reign lasted a mere three months, or a month, or even a week. After that, they found themselves eclipsed by a rival who was neither more beautiful nor younger nor richer, but to whom, for trivial reasons, indeed for no reason at all, fashion passed the torch.

And carefree, excited, all bedecked in flowers and gauze, in silk and fur, she accepts this torch without realizing what a burden it will be, unaware of all its pitfalls.

Do you know what a fashionable woman is? Do you know how she acquires this title? Do you know what it exposes her to? You're about to find out.

Imagine seven or eight scatterbrains,[1] but friendly scatterbrains, the well-mannered ones, who hide their good education with as much zeal as others hide their absurdity, the kind of scatterbrain who wears silk stockings, a small lorgnon, and yellow gloves.[2] So these seven or eight scatterbrains decide to adopt a woman. There they are: extolling her, gathering around her, following her everywhere, reading, in the glances she casually casts, the wishes they eagerly grant. In short, out of one hundred women, they see but one.

At the Opéra and Bouffes,[3] the seven or eight scatterbrains barge into her box all at once under the pretext of greeting her. They talk loudly while she laughs and make

---

[1] Foa constructs the image of the elegant woman as seen through the eyes of fashionable high-society men.

[2] Yellow gloves were a coveted fashion accessory and a sign of distinction. There are many references to yellow gloves in literature and in the visual culture of the period, including in Balzac's *Le père Goriot* (*Old Goriot*).

[3] Popular Parisian theaters frequented by fashionable society.

all the men in the orchestra seats turn their heads, first because they are upset about the noise, but then because they are intrigued by the sight of a beautiful woman. And that makes everyone ask: "Who is this woman? — Madame So-and-So! What, you haven't heard? She is the most fashionable woman in Paris. —But I don't believe she is the most beautiful one. —I didn't say the most beautiful, I said the most fashionable, which is not at all the same thing. —Oh, pardon me, I didn't know that. — This gentleman is from the provinces, says one man to his neighbor. —Or an Algerian,"[4] this neighbor replies with a smile.

The fashionable woman's time is short. In order to obtain this title, there's no need to be a duchess, a marquise, a countess, or any other titled nobility; in fact, what's better than having all those titles is having a stockbroker for a husband. Oh, the stockbroker husband is the husband par excellence, a model husband, a romantic husband.

A stockbroker husband makes so much money, so easily, so simply, and so rapidly, that in truth he'd have to be worse than a rentier[5] to refuse his wife fineries: a piece

---

[4] In 1833 Algeria was a popular topic of conversation; France began its Algerian conquest in 1830.

[5] A rentier was a man who lived off the revenues of his business or property but who himself did not have to work. He was often an object of derision in the literature of the time.

of jewelry or an outfit that he can pay for with what he earns in mere seconds with the simple stroke of a pen.

It is also true that it can only take a second for him to lose the fruits of a whole year's worth of pen strokes. But what can you do? That's the other side of the coin. *gambled*
fortunes

But let me get back to my topic from which I digress—my apologies.

So, to be a fashionable woman, and I assure you, this is not so easy, you have to be a little older than twenty, a little younger than thirty; you can be fat or thin, blonde or brunette, or have light-brown hair; in fact, hair color doesn't really matter (with the exception of redheads). But the brunette will last a few hours longer than the blonde.

The fashionable woman is always dressed with simplicity and elegance, she never wears any jewelry—she has the foresight to keep it for when her reign is over, to get herself noticed.

The fashionable woman buys her hats at Simon, her bonnets at Herbeault, her shoes at Michaël, her boots at Gélot, her gloves at Boivins. She only wears flowers from Batton and feathers from Cartier.[6]

The fashionable woman is not herself a seamstress but rather the one who comes up with or improves the cut of

---

[6] Well-regarded and sought-after producers of articles of high fashion who established fashion trends in Paris and in other cities seeking to emulate Parisian women.

a new dress; however, she will, though only once (please note: just once), have a dress made by Madame Palmyre,[7] but never two. Madame Palmyre repeats herself, and it is most unfortunate to see three other dresses that resemble yours while out at a ball. It's enough to make your head spin.

The fashionable woman arrives at the ball. No sooner has she stepped out of her carriage than she is asked to dance. She is asked on the staircase, on the landing; she was asked yesterday, the day before yesterday, at the previous ball. She has more invitations upon entering the ballroom than there will be contredanses[8] to dance the entire night.

And so the awkward admirer who approaches her as soon as she arrives will find himself with the following reply: "My dance card is already full. —How about the second dance? —It's already taken, Monsieur. —What about the third? —I've already promised the first ten. I doubt I will be able to do more than that. —So, Madame, may I have the pleasure of a waltz? —I am taken for all

---

[7] Madame Palmyre was a famous dressmaker. The Empress Eugénie, a fashion trendsetter and the wife of Napoleon III, later became one of her clients.

[8] The contredanse, originating from the English "country dance," is a type of dance in which couples face each other in two lines. It was popular among the French aristocracy and bourgeoisie in the eighteenth and nineteenth centuries.

of them. —May I have the pleasure of a gallop?[9] —I will dance only one gallop, and my partner is right here! — What terrible luck, Madame!" And the unfortunate man goes on sighing, and the lady goes on not paying him the slightest bit of attention.

Then the fashionable woman finds herself surrounded to the point of not being able to breathe, sought after to the point of not knowing whom to answer first, suffocated by compliments (if compliments can suffocate) and intoxicated by incense (incense can intoxicate). It's all very charming.

She stays at the ball only for a little while, like a flash of lightning, just enough time to dazzle, and that's it. She repeats this same act at two or three other balls, then leaves, goes home early, well before the fatigue or the dancing dims the twinkle in her eyes, uncurls her hair, and deshines her dress.[10]

One must be able to say about her, "She only came for a minute, she had so many invitations, so many social obligations to fulfill, you could barely catch a glimpse of her. But never was she prettier than tonight!"

Whatever night that was.

---

[9] A lively dance with a two-beat rhythm, orginally from Hungary but eventually made popular in France.

[10] Here Foa uses the neologism *débrillanter*, related to *briller* (to shine, to gleam), both literally and figuratively.

The fashionable woman gets up late and spends her mornings at home. She takes care of her household, unless she has a mother or mother-in-law to do that; or she takes care of her children, if she has any; or she paints and plays music, because in the nineteenth century, women do all that, and they admit it. They are well brought up, have many talents, especially in painting and music. Moving on.

Around four in the afternoon, she gets into her carriage, and where does it take her? To the park, of course, next to the entrance where a horse is waiting (or not waiting), a horse saddled just for her, held by her well-dressed servant, who himself is on a beautiful horse. Next to her prance a few gentlemen, the dancers from the day before, those scatterbrains you have already met.

And if the weather is bad? Madame goes on visits or shopping. Or maybe she goes to see the latest art exhibit.

Then dinner, then the Opéra or Bouffes, from there to the ball, and so on and so forth, until the spring, the time when every self-respecting woman, every woman who cares about her reputation, leaves Paris for the countryside. She only returns, fresher and more beautiful than ever, at the beginning of winter.

Poor thing! Sadly, her place is now taken, her throne is occupied, her scepter is broken, her reign is finished. She is nevertheless more fortunate than dethroned kings for, unlike them, she is not exiled. She can still visit the scenes of her glory, she can enjoy the success of a rival, or she can die of jealousy, as she wishes. She can try, if that's her fancy, to once again explore that moving terrain of studied glances, diaphanous smiles, sparkling words; oh well!

No more stampede in her theater box; the box is full, but the door is closed. No more crowds of dancers at the ball. The number of invitations equals that of the dances, perhaps sometimes one more. No more dust swirling around her carriage when it goes to the park—just enough to get in your eyes, and that's all. It's a disaster.

If the husband of the aforementioned fashionable woman has kept his fortune (which is rare these days, I assure you), the most outrageous luxury, the most exquisite outfit will still bring some attention to her. But people will whisper, loudly enough so that she can hear, "This is Madame So-and-So, the one who was all the rage last year, the fashionable woman of that time. Today she is merely one of our elegant women."

But if her husband has lost his fortune, which is likely (a year is a long time for a Parisian fortune), and if some old men with failing memories go on to ask someone fashionable, "Tell me, my friend, whatever happened to Madame So-and-So? —Madame So-and-So . . . honestly, I have no idea who you're talking about. —Bah! My word. —Wait, was that the cute blonde (or brunette) who would dance with no one but you? —Ah, yes, I re- member her now! —Her husband is ruined, isn't he? . . . Honestly, I don't know whatever became of her; one no longer sees her anywhere. Oh, but forgive me, here is the divinity *du jour*, and I have an engagement with her."

And the forgetful character is all bows and smiles. The same glances, the same words bestowed last year are now destined for the fashionable woman of the moment.

Tell me, is it really worth all the work, all the exhaus- tion, all the heartache, just to be named fashionable woman for maybe six months, only to see yourself, a year later, either forgotten, or delegated to the ranks of "elegant" women? She is lucky if a fluxion of the chest or cholera does not put an end to such brilliant success.

Goodness me, I think it's better to enjoy oneself with- out being too splashy, to please without dazzling, to inspire neither envy nor pity, to eclipse no one even if one risks being a little eclipsed oneself, and simply to be charming. What do you think?

Not just anyone can be a fashionable woman.

I am not sure, but some say that this last reflection may soothe fashionable women, and console those who no longer are.

Eugène Scribe and Henri Dupin
The Stockbroker's Son

This play is emblematic of the popular theatrical works of the mid nineteenth century. These examples of commercial bourgeois culture featured stereotypical characters and formulaic plots and often incorporated humorous songs set to popular tunes. The stockbroker was a bourgeois type that was featured in other urban studies from the nineteenth century, including The French Depicted by Themselves.

DALOGNY, stockbroker

HORTENSE, Dalogny's wife

THÉOPHILE, cabinetmaker

JOSÉPHINE, Hortense's servant

DUMONT, Dalogny's servant

Paris: In the home of Monsieur Dalogny

A room with a door in the back and side doors in the foreground. To the left, a table covered by a tablecloth; to the right, a cradle; in the back, a dresser.

SCENE 1

JOSÉPHINE, *sitting by the cradle*

(To the tune of "L'oiseau bleu"[1])
JOSÉPHINE, *getting up.*
He's quieting down, thankfully
All day this mean little baby
Has been pushing me to the brink
He keeps causing such a stink!
In your bed *(repeat)*
Rest your dear head
Babies are so sweet
When they are fast asleep!

(She looks in the cradle.)
It's a stroke of fate
He's resting—how great!
Now I'll daydream of my boyfriend
And get a little rest on my end.
In your bed . . . *(etc.)*

All day, at his beck and call. And, as if things in this
house weren't enough already—what with obeying
the orders of Monsieur and Madame—now there is
a third little bourgeois who whines even more than

---

[1] "L'oiseau bleu" was a popular song. Vaudevilles often contained
songs with lyrics set to existing popular melodies, sometimes from
other vaudevilles.

the other two! Even more so now that there are marital issues afoot: Monsieur wants his son to have a wet nurse; Madame is opposed to it.[2] And now we have an heir who, with thirty thousand livres of income, risks dying of hunger (*running to the cradle*). Oh, my God! . . . I thought he woke up . . . no, no, thank goodness . . . I never have a moment to myself.

> (*To the tune of "Ave Maria"*)
> Sleep tight, baby, sleep tight,
> It's my motto, throughout the day,
> It's the one I have to say,
> So the baby will go night-night.
>
> We take such good care
> Every day we put down to rest
> Others' children everywhere
> I wonder what that might suggest . . .
>
> Sleep tight, baby, sleep tight.

SCENE 2

THÉOPHILE, *entering rapidly*, JOSÉPHINE

JOSÉPHINE. Who's there? Could it be? Monsieur Théophile . . . in this house?!

---

[2] In the nineteenth century, well-off families employed a wet nurse in their home if the mother chose not to breastfeed her children.

THÉOPHILE, *in a determined tone.* Yes, ma'am. I left the
   faubourg Saint-Antoine,[3] I left my boutique, my job as
   cabinetmaker.

JOSÉPHINE. But why?

THÉOPHILE. To see you . . . I can't take it anymore.

   (To the tune of "A l'âge heureux de quatorze ans")
   So I come; here I am . . .

JOSÉPHINE.
   Oh, my! Are you crazy?
   What? Coming here, on a Tuesday?
   But it's not a holiday.

THÉOPHILE.
   It's too much for me; each day
   I have to pour my heart out
   My love cannot wait until Sunday
   Is that truly my fault?

It's too long . . . and even on Sundays . . . I don't get to see
   you . . . Did you come the day before yesterday? . . .
   Didn't I wait for you the whole night at the Colysée?[4]

JOSÉPHINE. What was I supposed I do? This little one
   does nothing but cry . . . I couldn't leave him.

---

[3] A traditionally working-class neighborhood, the faubourg Saint-
Antoine links what is now the Place de la Bastille with the Place de la
Nation. It was known as the furniture-making district of Paris, a sig-
nificant detail here because Théophile is employed as a cabinetmaker.

[4] A popular working-class dance hall.

THÉOPHILE. The little one! The little one! What do I care about the little one? Do you think I'm going to let him boss me around? No, gadzooks!

JOSÉPHINE. Be quiet!

THÉOPHILE, *raising his voice.* If you want to talk about crying . . . I'll cry . . . even louder than him . . . I'm not afraid.

JOSÉPHINE. You wouldn't dare.

THÉOPHILE. What do you want, Joséphine? I can't help myself. You, you are cold and indifferent. You don't know what kind of passion dwells in the mind of a young person or in the heart of a cabinetmaker. Passion, you see, is a sentiment that means that I'm there, in my boutique, like a fool . . . not knowing if I'm holding the arm of a chair or the neck of a swan. I think I'm working, and I am not. And I tell myself, "That little Joséphine, whom I have known for so long . . . with whom I grew up in the country . . . who is the maid of a stockbroker in the Chaussée d'Antin[5] . . . and who may have dozens of lovers hanging around her at all times, while I'm hanging around table legs or writing desks . . ." At the mere thought, my heart starts to beat, blood rushes to my head, my hand starts to move, and I break the furniture.

---

[5] A neighborhood in Paris (in what is now the ninth arrondissement) inhabited by the upwardly mobile bourgeoisie (such as Madame de Nucingen, a wealthy banker's wife in Balzac's *Le père Goriot* [*Old Goriot*]).

JOSÉPHINE. What a mess!

THÉOPHILE. Because of that, I get nothing from my master on Saturday. On the other hand, all week long, I get beaten.

JOSÉPHINE. My poor Théophile.

THÉOPHILE. I don't even feel it. I am thinking of you . . . that stops me from returning the blows. But one day, I won't be so careful . . . I'll kill him! It's certain! I am capable of it!

JOSÉPHINE. Oh, my God!

THÉOPHILE. So, to avoid any trouble, I want to leave my job.

JOSÉPHINE. What madness!

THÉOPHILE. It's no longer worth it. The modern cabinetmaker is crushed . . . with what people are asking for these days—those medieval-looking dressers and Pompadour beds.[6]

JOSÉPHINE. That's news to me!

THÉOPHILE. It's old news! Especially the Pompadour beds. I don't know what they do with them—there are no used pieces of furniture like that. So I have decided—I'm resigning, and I'm going to be like you, ma'am . . . I'm becoming a domestic servant.

JOSÉPHINE. Sacrificing your freedom!

-----

[6] A curved bed frame inspired by the one in the bedroom of Madame de Pompadour (Louis XV's mistress) at Versailles.

THÉOPHILE. My freedom! That's what's forcing me to go hungry . . . and to be on the receiving end of blows! Who wants that? I'll give it up—for good wages, good dinners, and a place near you.

JOSÉPHINE. Near me?

THÉOPHILE. Of course! You must get me hired here as a countinghouse clerk . . . a manservant . . . even a porter. You told me that Madame fired hers. A porter with a plume . . . and a sword . . . it's so lovely and seductive . . . that would seduce you, I'm sure of it.

> *(To the tune of the "Vaudeville de Fanchon")*
> A haughty air
> An epaulette[7]
> A plume, an aiguillette[8]
> That's almost an officer
> An officer who's debonair
> Who, to take the greatest care,
> Always stays closely by,
> With a sword by his side.

(Assuming the position of a manservant behind a carriage)

JOSÉPHINE. Yes, certainly, it would be a great job, but not in this house.

THÉOPHILE. But why?

---

[7] An ornamental shoulder piece worn on a coat, often by members of the military.

[8] Braided loops that ornament military uniforms.

JOSÉPHINE. Monsieur would never want you here, Théophile.

THÉOPHILE. He doesn't know me. You never let me come here.

JOSÉPHINE. With good reason.

THÉOPHILE. For what reason? I'm attractive . . . I'm nice . . . I look presentable.

JOSÉPHINE. As we know all too well.

THÉOPHILE. Is it a fault?

JOSÉPHINE. It can be.

THÉOPHILE. What does that mean?

JOSÉPHINE. I am not going to say, but for my sake, and possibly yours too, please do not try to get a job in this house. You've already been here long enough, in fact, and if you love me, Théophile . . .

THÉOPHILE. If I love you?

JOSÉPHINE. You will go right away.

THÉOPHILE. Go! Be careful, Joséphine . . . Something is going on here, and I'm going to figure out . . . you don't know me . . . you don't know what the faubourg Saint-Antoine[9] is capable of . . . when I am in love . . . I am capable of getting a job here . . . in spite of you . . . and in spite of your bosses . . . I'll find a way.

JOSÉPHINE. You wouldn't dare . . .

---

[9] A working-class neighborhood in the eastern part of Paris.

THÉOPHILE. I certainly would dare . . . I would dare it all . . . because I'm bold and imaginative. Once you've lost your head, what else is there to lose?

JOSÉPHINE. What about the risks?

THÉOPHILE. I don't care.

JOSÉPHINE. And my honor?

THÉOPHILE. That I do care about . . . because I am marrying you!

JOSÉPHINE. If I say yes . . .

THÉOPHILE. You will . . . or I'll throw myself out the window!

JOSÉPHINE. Have you ever seen the like? . . . Oh, my God! Someone's coming . . . get out, sir!

THÉOPHILE. I won't leave before you answer me. (*insisting*) The door or the window—you choose!

JOSÉPHINE. But it's detestable to impose yourself on someone like this.

THÉOPHILE. I'll impose myself on the door or the window . . . you choose.

JOSÉPHINE. Fine! The door!

THÉOPHILE. What a relief.

(*He goes to leave through the back.*)

JOSÉPHINE, *stopping him.* Not that one! You'll be seen by the people in the office. (*showing him to the left*) Go this way instead—a hidden stairway that leads to Rue Taitbout.

THÉOPHILE. Where my aunt works next door as *portière*[10] . . . I'll move into her place.

JOSÉPHINE, *who has gone next to the left-hand door.* Will you just leave! (*Looking around*) That's no longer possible . . . Monsieur is coming up this way . . . don't let him see you (*She goes to the back.*)—and with Germain in the antechamber, where will you hide?

THÉOPHILE. Wherever you want . . . I don't care . . . in the cradle?

JOSÉPHINE, *angrily.* The baby's cradle . . .

THÉOPHILE, *showing a table to the left.* There . . . under that table.

JOSÉPHINE. Impossible.

THÉOPHILE, *getting down there.* Here I am! A mahogany table! I feel right at home.*

JOSÉPHINE, *lowering the tablecloth.* Be quiet now!

(She sits near the table and embroiders.)

---

* The actor is meant to be under the table; but he leaves through a trapdoor, which gives him more time to get dressed and to reappear as a woman in scene 4. [Note in original text.]

---

[10] The *portier* or *portière* (the female version of this type) is an employee of an apartment building who lives by the entrance and is in charge of keeping order in the building. In popular culture, the *portier* or *portière* is seen as a figure who polices the comings and goings as well as the behavior of the residents.

SCENE 3

THÉOPHILE, *under the table,*
JOSÉPHINE, DALOGNY

DALOGNY. I had some time to run an errand and make my morning purchases . . . no one even saw me leave . . . Oh! There you are, my little Joséphine.

JOSÉPHINE, *disconcerted*. Yes, sir.

DALOGNY. Is my wife up?

JOSÉPHINE, *distressed*. No, sir . . . I mean . . . I don't know . . . you could go see her.

DALOGNY. Oh, well, of course . . . all I need to do is wake her up . . . it would cause quite a scene.

> *(To the tune of "J'en guette un petit de mon âge")*
> Waking up a young mother
> Who is nursing and not sleeping
> Would mean tears like no other
> And, my dear, nonstop weeping;
> Alas, I can tell what the price will be
> In such a case to dry those tears,
> A tissue is hardly enough, I fear,
> I'll need a cashmere as my fee.

Nothing is as precious as a young mother . . . maternal tenderness is so whimsical . . . As for you, my little Joséphine, you unfortunately have no such whimsy.

JOSÉPHINE, *prudishly*. What do you mean?

DALOGNY.   I mean that you are the nicest servant . . . the most fiery . . . and if you could just like me a bit more than you do now . . .

JOSÉPHINE, *loudly, in order to be heard by Théophile.* But I don't like you at all.

DALOGNY.   Come on . . . you say that today . . .

JOSÉPHINE.   I say it every day.

DALOGNY.   For now . . . but that won't last . . . You know, my dear, that I promised you a dowry . . . if you were well-behaved . . .

JOSÉPHINE, *pushing the table toward the door on the right-hand side.* And you know better than anyone that I deserve it.

DALOGNY.   That depends!

JOSÉPHINE.   What do you mean, sir . . . "that depends!"

DALOGNY.   I really mean it.

JOSÉPHINE, *aside.* Can't he just spit it out?

DALOGNY.   Why on earth do you keep pushing that table toward the door? No one will be able to get in . . . or out! Come here, listen to me. You know, Joséphine, that I like virtue . . . especially when it comes to my servants . . . and I won't stand for anyone in the pantry making eyes at you.

JOSÉPHINE.   And who would dare to do that?

DALOGNY.   Anatole, my former porter, whom I fired for that very reason.

JOSÉPHINE. Bah! I promise you that you were mistaken.

DALOGNY. It's possible . . . but from now on . . . I don't want any good-looking, well-built young men in my home. Those swindlers can really wreck a home . . . often they are confused with their masters . . . if it weren't for the yellow gloves.[11] Now yellow gloves are the only thing establishing the hierarchy of our civilization! (*taking off his gloves*) . . . take them off—everything is equalized . . . mixed up . . . it's just what I was saying earlier at the Café Tortoni.[12] But back to you . . . my little Joséphine . . . whose values I know. We will only have old men here like Dumont the man-servant . . . or those going through their second childhood between the ages of forty-five and fifty years old.

JOSÉPHINE, *aside.* Poor Théophile . . .

DALOGNY. And if you stay well behaved . . . I will keep my word. I will give you a nice dowry . . . five to six thousand francs.

JOSÉPHINE. Really!

DALOGNY. Only on one condition . . .

---

[11] Yellow gloves were a coveted fashion accessory and a sign of distinction. There are many references to yellow gloves in literature and in the visual culture of the period, including in Balzac's *Old Goriot*.

[12] Situated on the Boulevard des Italiens, the Café Tortoni was dubbed an "établissement de luxe ouvert à tous" 'a luxury establishment open to all' and indeed was frequented by people of differing social ranks.

JOSÉPHINE. What condition?

DALOGNY. That you never get married.

JOSÉPHINE. Well, I never!

DALOGNY. It's in your best interest, because a chambermaid who is not married, that's better . . . it's just better. Mademoiselle Joséphine . . . it's distinguished . . . but Madame Dumont . . . or Madame Dubois . . . it's bourgeois . . . it's Rue Saint-Denis[13] . . . I wouldn't want that . . . my wife wouldn't either . . . but, on the other hand, my sweet child, you will find a certain compensation in the affection of your masters.

JOSÉPHINE. You think so?

DALOGNY. And to prove it to you (showing her a parcel he placed on a chair when entering) . . . Look! . . . here you go!

(To the tune of the "Vaudeville de l'Apothicaire")
A silk dress. . .

JOSÉPHINE, opening the parcel.
Yes, it's true.

DALOGNY.
To reward your skill and zeal,
I just bought this for you,
From the shopkeeper Delille.

JOSÉPHINE.
This is lilac satin, how grand . . .

---

[13] A street in a working-class neighborhood.

(*Aside, subtly*)
When we go out on a date
And he gives me his hand
Théophile will think this is great!

DALOGNY.
Try it on, we haven't got all day
On your finger, you sneaky thing!

JOSÉPHINE.
No, no, sir, what will people say?
(*looking*) I think this is a turquoise ring.

DALOGNY.
With diamonds.

JOSÉPHINE.
It's exquisite!

DALOGNY.
I just want you to obey me. (*He puts the ring on her finger.*)

JOSÉPHINE, *aside.*
When he kisses my hand, Théophile will lose his mind!

DALOGNY. And if you think it's too much . . . all you owe me in return . . . and all I ask for . . . is that you listen to me a bit.

JOSÉPHINE, *defending herself with difficulty and still looking to the side of the table.* Think of it . . . a respectable man.

DALOGNY. What does that have to do with it?

JOSÉPHINE. A stockbroker . . .

DALOGNY. All the more reason . . .

JOSÉPHINE. Who has such a lovely wife.

DALOGNY. Bah! . . . a wife who is nursing . . . and to whom I can never talk without her replying about maternal love . . . it's boring . . . and so on and so forth . . . I have therefore decided to hire a wet nurse.

JOSÉPHINE. Is that possible?

DALOGNY. Who was recommended to me by Gervault, my farmer from Poissy.[14]

JOSÉPHINE. Will Madame agree to it?

DALOGNY. She had better . . .

HORTENSE, *offstage.* Ah! it's terrible! . . . it's tyrannical!

DALOGNY. Shush, here she comes.

JOSÉPHINE, *aside, still pushing the table against the right-hand door.* Will he have had the sense to go out through the stairs? I don't even dare look.

SCENE 4

JOSÉPHINE, DALOGNY, HORTENSE

HORTENSE, *with a letter in hand.* Well, I never . . . we will see about this . . .

DALOGNY. Oh, my God! Madame, what is going on?

---

[14] A town to the west of Paris.

HORTENSE. What is going on, sir . . . without warning me . . . without consulting me . . . such an action . . . this letter from your farmer Gervault.

DALOGNY. You read a letter addressed to me?

HORTENSE. Why not? You certainly read mine. For example the one yesterday . . . from a young clerk . . . an unimportant note.

DALOGNY. If you like . . .

HORTENSE. Yes, if you'd like to misinterpret it. Whereas this one . . . it's clear . . . it's obvious . . . Gervaut apologizes for not yet having sent you the wet nurse that you asked him for. A wet nurse! Here! And why, may I ask?

DALOGNY. It is in your best interest . . . my love . . . in the interest of your health.

HORTENSE. To separate me from my son?

DALOGNY. I am worried that it is tiring you out.

HORTENSE. But it's natural, sir!

DALOGNY. And the balls at the Opéra . . . which you seem incapable of giving up. Do you think those are also natural?

HORTENSE. Certainly . . . because my doctors have recommended entertainment and pleasure. They are recommending that I avoid irritants and annoyances . . . and you are always there . . . opposing what my doctor prescribes . . . (*crying*) Wanting to entrust my children . . . to a stranger . . . to a hired hand!

DALOGNY. A hired hand who gets up every day at seven
   in the morning and goes to bed at eight at night is better than a young mother who goes out every night.

>   *(To the tune of "Que d'établissements nouveaux")*
>   As for me, this is what I think . . .

HORTENSE.
I am seething with anger!
You want to hand our son
Over to a complete stranger!
We want this child, later on
To love his parents, to care . . .

DALOGNY.
Yes, exactly . . .
When he finds out that, for their heir
They paid the wet nurse's fee!

HORTENSE. And you think that I will tolerate that . . .
   that I will let myself be dispossessed of my rights.

DALOGNY. Listen to that language . . . that is Jean-
   Jacques, plain and simple.[15] I found one of his volumes
   the other day on your dressing table.

JOSÉPHINE, *who walks near the cradle to the left and sits
   down.* That book that Madame reads every morning
   while we do her hair.

-----

[15] Jean-Jacques Rousseau, in his 1762 work *Émile*, advocated that
women breastfeed their own children.

HORTENSE. Yes, sir . . . an admirable man.

DALOGNY. Admirable in his prose . . . but not in his actions.

HORTENSE. He understood children's education, at any rate.

DALOGNY. That's why he left his own at the orphanage. I am not so great a philosopher, yet I will settle for leaving my children with a wet nurse.

HORTENSE. You need my consent.

DALOGNY. And you will give it . . . because we are leaving here in two weeks. We have a trip to take for the estate of your uncle.

HORTENSE. You can go alone.

DALOGNY. Absolutely not.

HORTENSE. I will stay in Paris.

DALOGNY. Very well . . . if that is what you want . . . to stay here among your admirers . . . no one to get in the way of their compliments . . . to entertain that young clerk.

HORTENSE. Monsieur Melval.

DALOGNY. The one who was asking you for a meeting yesterday?

HORTENSE. For a business affair.

DALOGNY. A love affair . . . because he loves you.

HORTENSE. He's never told me that.

DALOGNY. Well! He told it to me . . . at the last ball at the Opéra. He was disguised . . . as was I. He took me for one of his friends, and he confided in me about his love for you. He was waiting, he said, for the right moment to declare it to you.

HORTENSE. Oh, really . . . well! I didn't know. I am hearing it here for the first time.

DALOGNY. God! What a blunder! All the more reason to bring you with me . . . and I cannot take you with me while you are still nursing.

HORTENSE. Well, that is why you've requested a wet nurse . . . out of jealousy.

DALOGNY. Jealousy or not . . . we must hire her when she arrives.

HORTENSE. But she is not coming. Gervault says she is seriously indisposed.

DALOGNY. Well, then! We will find another, just go to the Rue Sainte-Apolline to the wet nurses' office.[16]

HORTENSE. How awful!

DALOGNY. The most wonderful of institutions.

(To the tune of "Adieu, je vous fuis, bois charmans")
Defended by authority
Of laws protective, not perverse,

---

[16] Wet nurses often came from the country to work for the wealthier women of Paris, and the wet nurses' office regulated their services.

You must know that humanity
Has created the office of the wet nurse.
Its success is always constant
On antiquity it's based
Because it's an establishment
To which civilization's traced!

SCENE 5

DALOGNY, DUMONT, HORTENSE,
JOSÉPHINE, *at the cradle.*

DUMONT.   Oh! Sir . . . sir, here she is!

DALOGNY.   Who?

DUMONT.   She will make you happy . . . you just have to see her. She looks so healthy . . . and with a very refined stoutness.

DALOGNY.   But who are you talking about?

DUMONT.   The person you were waiting for . . . told me to welcome.

HORTENSE.   Can't you just say it?

DUMONT.   The wet nurse!

DALOGNY.   The wet nurse . . . (*looking with satisfaction at Hortense*) Now there's no going back on it.

SCENE 6

THE SAME; THÉOPHILE, *disguised as
a wet nurse, enters.* DUMONT *points out
DALOGNY to* THÉOPHILE. THÉOPHILE
*steps forward and curtsies; he is holding
a small package under his left arm.*

JOSÉPHINE, *aside.* Oh, God! Théophile!

*(To the tune of "Jeunes beautés, charmantes
demoiselles")*
THÉOPHILE.
The boss! A blessing, not a curse!
Good sir, I have come here
To serve and tend, as his wet nurse,
Your son, so young and dear.
What fortune and success
He'll have, and be a ladies' man,
If he turns out just as well dressed
And suave as his old man.

Together, aside
DALOGNY.
This wet nurse looks so plump and well
Oh my, oh my, how glorious!
My wife, I know, will be in hell
And I will be victorious.

JOSÉPHINE.
So the wet nurse is Théophile—
How reckless, how insane!

This scene, which seems to him ideal,
Is causing me much pain!

HORTENSE.
So she is here, this new wet nurse—
And what should I do now?
Oh, dear, her presence is a curse;
Monsieur is proud, and how.

THÉOPHILE.
Oh, what a blessing, not a curse!
I have just gotten here
To serve and tend, as his wet nurse,
This boy, so young and dear.

DUMONT.
Oh, what a blessing, not a curse!
Now here she is—how charming!
This lovely woman, the wet nurse—
She is so plump and darling.

(At the refrain, Théophile curtsies to everyone. Hortense turns away angrily, as does Joséphine. Théophile gives his package to Dumont, who places it on the dresser.)

DALOGNY. Gervault told us that you were unwell . . .
You are doing better, then?

THÉOPHILE. Much better, so I set out right away.*

---

* In this part, Théophile must speak with a female voice, with the garrulousness and persnicketiness of a wet nurse. [Note in original text.]

DALOGNY, *to Hortense.* I hope, Madame, that my farmer Gervault did not mislead us, and that he has sent us a lovely wet nurse.

HORTENSE. We will have to see.

JOSÉPHINE. I agree with Madame. We cannot carelessly let in . . .

HORTENSE. Joséphine is right.

DALOGNY. Why is she meddling in this affair?

THÉOPHILE. Actually, I think that, in fact, mademoiselle doesn't really know . . . and unless she has specific reasons for wanting to drive me away . . .

JOSÉPHINE. Me?

THÉOPHILE. I know all too well that in households the maids get angry at the wet nurses . . . who are the real victims. (*crying*) And it is very sad knowing that while we are giving life to our masters, our own life will be so difficult.

DALOGNY. Now, now . . . calm down.

THÉOPHILE. I've lived through so many humiliations . . . because I'm an expert when it comes to nourishment.

DALOGNY. This is not your first child, then?

THÉOPHILE. I've had five: an ironworker, a deputy prosecutor, a colonel, a Peer of France, and a shopkeeper.

DALOGNY, *to Hortense.* You can see she is well informed.

THÉOPHILE. And oh, is it ever sweet, several years later, to tell myself, as I see a magistrate or a police captain walking by, that I held in my arms, that I raised, nursed, whipped . . . those rascals . . . those are the life pleasures of a wet nurse. And a wet nurse deserves some kind of recompense because, despite her heart and her husband, her situation forces upon her strict norms of conduct. It's not about me. I would think nothing of it all . . . everyone would tell you that.

DALOGNY. I don't doubt it. What is your name?

THÉOPHILE. Marie-Madelaine . . .

DALOGNY. Gervault told me Mitonneau.

THÉOPHILE. Marie-Madelaine, wife of Mitonneau, Monsieur Mitonneau, of Poissy, keeper of livestock. Employed by the administration of horned beasts. And, despite what the jokers of the area might say, there is no need to confuse him with his constituents. Because I am known in these parts, as is he, and this morning, when he kissed me while putting me into the *coucou* . . .[17]

DALOGNY. The *coucou*?

----

[17] A *coucou* was a small vehicle for hire pulled by one horse, in use since the eighteenth century. There are several uses of wordplay in this section. First, "Madame Mitonneau" explains that her husband works with animals but uses administrative language to do so. Second, her mention of horned beasts, or "bêtes à cornes," evokes the idea of a cuckold husband. Finally, the word *coucou* sounds like the French *cocu*, or cuckold, and confuses Dalogny. What Théophile is joking about here is that, despite what some might say, Mr. Mitonneau has not been cuckolded.

THÉOPHILE. Yes, sir . . . a very sturdy carriage . . . for modesty . . . especially when one is in the front seat and in the company of cattle salesmen. No one is as crude as a cattle salesman. I mean crude in their language, because, well, you know . . .

DALOGNY. It goes without saying . . . Well, then! Madame Mitonneau, starting today you will be part of our household.

JOSÉPHINE, *aside*. Oh, my God!

HORTENSE. Not yet. I have not yet said that this wet nurse suits me. I want my doctor's opinion, and according to him . . .

THÉOPHILE, *aside, in his masculine voice*. Of course you do! A young doctor, completely loyal to you, who will say whatever you want him to. But I'll have my doctor come too . . . and he's an old one.

JOSÉPHINE. Two doctors!

DALOGNY. And I will only trust his opinion that will surely be a favorable one for Madame Mitonneau if you can believe your eyes . . . and before then, I insist that she start work immediately. Go ahead, Wet Nurse, you heard me . . . take the baby.

HORTENSE. I object!

JOSÉPHINE. Madame is right.

HORTENSE: Before anything else, I need to talk to this wet nurse. (*aside*) After that, we will see if she remains. (*out loud*) You won't be so cruel to refuse me that satisfaction.

(To the tune of "Lestocq")
DALOGNY.
It's what Madame desires
And her wishes are my own;
What else would I require?
So this meeting I condone.

THÉOPHILE, *to Joséphine.*
She's making him retreat
And the reason must surely be . . .

JOSÉPHINE, *to Théophile.*
She wants to throw you on the street
And with that I agree.

Together
THÉOPHILE.
The husband is retreating;
His wish is her wish too.
I'm fearful of this meeting—
What will she tell me to do?

HORTENSE.
My husband is retreating;
This is all well and nice.
I'm going to get my meeting
And I think that should suffice.

(Dalogny exits through the back and Joséphine through the right door that leads to Hortense's room. Théophile goes to the cradle.)

SCENE 7

HORTENSE, THÉOPHILE

HORTENSE. Come close, Madame Mitonneau, and if you're smart, you'll listen carefully to what I am about to tell you.

THÉOPHILE. Yes, Madame.

HORTENSE. To begin with, I don't want you here.

THÉOPHILE. Madame is very kind.

HORTENSE. And as long as you stay in this house, I will take it upon myself to make you so miserable that, within a few days, you will be tendering your resignation.

THÉOPHILE. I would never do that.

HORTENSE. Why?

THÉOPHILE. Because I will fit in wonderfully here.

HORTENSE. That's what we will have to see. To start, if you even touch my child, I will have you thrown out the window.

THÉOPHILE. You want to nurse him yourself?

HORTENSE. Yes, of course! Out of maternal love! And out of stubbornness.

THÉOPHILE. And you don't want me to nurse him?

HORTENSE. Never . . .

THÉOPHILE. Well, calm down, then . . . because that's also my intention.

HORTENSE. What are you saying?

THÉOPHILE. I won't give him a single drop of milk.

HORTENSE. Are you serious?

THÉOPHILE. I swear to it, and you can trust me, Marie-Madelaine, wife of Mitonneau, who has always been on the side of wives against their husbands. With couples, you just have to play nice so that the husbands don't figure anything out.

HORTENSE, *laughing*. Really! Is that what it's like in Poissy?

THÉOPHILE. And in Paris too. You know that no matter what, your husband will want to have a wet nurse. He is ornery, he is stubborn, and if you fire me, he will hire another one who won't work things out with you, who will want to do her own part, who, in a word, will want to perform her job as a wet nurse. Whereas for me, I don't care about it. I just care about pleasing you.

HORTENSE, *in a flattering tone*. This sweet little Madame Mitonneau.

THÉOPHILE. All I care about is serving you, because I have no desires of my own.

HORTENSE. Seriously?

THÉOPHILE. I told you that I was a different sort of woman.

HORTENSE. I can see that now! But how will we do this?

THÉOPHILE. Nothing could be simpler. When the baby cries, I will bring him to you in secret, sneakily. This way, you will have a wet nurse . . .

HORTENSE. Who won't nurse . . .

THÉOPHILE. And I will have a job . . .

HORTENSE. That I will do . . .

THÉOPHILE. And I will make a salary . . .

HORTENSE, *smiling*. You see that from time to time . . . and the joy of pulling a fast one on my husband . . . of thwarting his tyranny . . . and, when I've made a fool of him . . . to eventually inform him . . .

THÉOPHILE. After quite some time.

HORTENSE. You are right. It will be lovely. And you'll never leave me. You'll stay here . . . close by me . . . and if you're discreet . . .

THÉOPHILE. I will be! You can count on me.

(*To the tune of "Une nuit au château"*)
HORTENSE.
I'll count on it and am at ease
Because I trust you, nurse
So let's go ahead and make peace
But come and kiss me first.

(*She kisses him.*)

SCENE 8

JOSÉPHINE, HORTENSE,
DALOGNY, THÉOPHILE

JOSÉPHINE.
What's happening . . . how can this be?

THÉOPHILE.
It's simple, dear; I'll tell you,
It means Madame appreciates me
And realizes my value.

Chorus
DALOGNY.
Good, she's docile and sensible
So we'll get down to business
In married life, on principle
You must rule with firmness.

ALL.
Good, she's docile and sensible
So we'll get down to business.

JOSÉPHINE. I can't get over it because of, well, I mean,
of what you were saying just a bit earlier.

HORTENSE. I've changed my mind. I had reservations
that I no longer have, because I am convinced now
that this is the wet nurse that I need.

JOSÉPHINE. Are you sure of it, Madame?

HORTENSE. Indeed. A respectable girl, whom I can completely trust.

JOSÉPHINE. But the essential qualities . . .

HORTENSE. She has very good milk.

JOSÉPHINE. The baby is going to starve if it only has that milk for lunch.

HORTENSE. She just gave him some in front of me.

JOSÉPHINE, *stunned*. In front of you?

HORTENSE. Well, why not? Why are you so surprised?

THÉOPHILE. It's true! What is wrong with this little chambermaid?

JOSÉPHINE, *insisting*. In front of you?

DALOGNY. And the little one?

THÉOPHILE. He loved it.

HORTENSE. And so, wet nurse, I will add to the wages that my husband is giving you. And I would also like to give you a dress—you know, Joséphine, my quilted coat that was twice my size?

JOSÉPHINE. That will never fit her.

HORTENSE. You will help her try it on later.

JOSÉPHINE. Me, Madame ? Well, I never . . . it's too much!

HORTENSE. But why? I intend for her to be served here as I am, that you be at her beck and call.

THÉOPHILE. You heard her. Just because I'm just a simple peasant, chambermaids always treat me condescendingly. Just because I am wearing this apron doesn't mean I don't have feelings. You'd best learn, missy, that this apron doesn't make the wearer. (*crying*) And it is very hard to endure such humiliation.

DALOGNY. Now, now, Nurse . . .

THÉOPHILE. Especially with such good masters. If only the servants were more like them, I would not cry with all the tears in my body like I am now.

HORTENSE. Look, now she is sobbing.

THÉOPHILE. I see that Mademoiselle Joséphine is mean-spirited and doesn't love her young master.

JOSÉPHINE. Me!

THÉOPHILE. And you don't like me either. Yes, you, missy, you don't like me, and you are always mad at me.

DALOGNY. I assure you she is not.

HORTENSE. Joséphine is a good girl with no hard feelings.

THÉOPHILE. Well, then, if that's true, she needs to prove it to me . . . by giving me a kiss.

JOSÉPHINE. Well! I never!

THÉOPHILE. You see . . . she's even prouder than Madame.

HORTENSE. She is right.

(*To the tune of "Il me faudra quitter l'empire"*)
DALOGNY.
This poor woman is sensitive, so deferential
To dry her tears . . . go kiss her.

JOSÉPHINE.
Sir, I think it is essential
That people appreciate good behavior
To receive such a favor.

DALOGNY.
Good! A woman . . .

HORTENSE.
Aha! Could it possibly be pride?

JOSÉPHINE.
If you only knew . . .

DALOGNY.
What excessive modesty! This is pushing
modesty to the extreme!

HORTENSE.
I kiss her without knowing her.

JOSÉPHINE, *aside.*
I don't kiss her because I do know her!

DALOGNY.   I command you to do it.

JOSÉPHINE.   As you wish, sir.

(*She goes to Théophile and kisses him.*)

THÉOPHILE.   It's about time! (*Joséphine moves away.*)
Now the other cheek.

DALOGNY, *bringing her back to Théophile.* Come on!

THÉOPHILE. It's very difficult. And still . . . what reluctance! Whereas I (*kissing her enthusiastically*) do it quite willingly.

DALOGNY. All right! Let's forget everything . . . and please, no more arguments. Where will you put this wet nurse?

HORTENSE. There's just one room . . . Joséphine's.

JOSÉPHINE. No, Madame . . . I don't want that.

HORTENSE. But why?

JOSÉPHINE. Why? Because, well . . . I like to be alone.

THÉOPHILE. What a cheeky, disagreeable little imp! Pooh! Missy, you should be ashamed of yourself.

JOSÉPHINE. But . . . if you only knew . . .

HORTENSE. I know that when you're a good colleague . . .

DALOGNY. You have to inconvenience yourself a little.

THÉOPHILE. Right . . . exactly what I was trying to say.

JOSÉPHINE. Do you have to be so insolent?!

THÉOPHILE. Me, insolent? Did you hear that? She calls me insolent. And you can attest to the fact that I wasn't even saying anything.

JOSÉPHINE. But, once again . . .

HORTENSE. Silence! And let's not get started again . . . she can stay with me, in my room . . . with my son . . . I prefer it.

JOSÉPHINE. But, Madame . . . You can't do that!

HORTENSE. And why not?

DALOGNY. What is wrong with her?

THÉOPHILE. Why is she getting involved?

DALOGNY. Silence! Once again . . . because you've just woken up the baby . . . and lest he start to cry . . . quickly nurse.

THÉOPHILE. Who?

DALOGNY. Take him . . . and nurse him.

THÉOPHILE. Oh, he'll be fine.

DALOGNY. It doesn't matter . . .

JOSÉPHINE, *ironically*. When you have so much milk, and such good milk, it should be a piece of cake.

THÉOPHILE. Certainly, it doesn't bother me at all, Miss Scandalmonger . . . and this poor little one . . . (*He goes to the cradle. Dalogny and Joséphine follow him there. He begins to take off his corset and looks at Dalogny.*) Oh, please, sir . . . if you only knew how sensitive I am, in terms of all this . . . well, that's just how we are in Poissy . . . I can't tolerate the presence of a man . . . or even a woman.

DALOGNY. Really?

THÉOPHILE. I am like that pot from the saying . . . I won't boil if I'm being watched . . . and all the emotion will dry up my milk.

HORTENSE. She is right.

DALOGNY. Nonetheless . . .

HORTENSE. Come on, sir . . . my son will cry. I'm going back into my room.

DALOGNY. And I am going back to my office. (*He leaves through the back.*)

HORTENSE. Please be so good as to give the wet nurse lunch.

THÉOPHILE. It's true! I'm starving!

HORTENSE. Everything she needs is here in the buffet, and you can bring up the wine.

JOSÉPHINE. Do wet nurses drink wine?

THÉOPHILE. Certainly . . . I don't want to put any water into my milk . . . the way they do in Paris. And, speaking of milk . . . some nice, hot coffee . . . I have some every day.

HORTENSE. Tell Dumont to bring her up some.

JOSÉPHINE. But, Madame . . .

HORTENSE. Go on . . . the wet nurse is waiting.

JOSÉPHINE, *stopping.* I would have been pleased to see . . .

THÉOPHILE, *imitating her.* Pleased to see . . . she is always talking back, this one . . . she doesn't know how to obey her masters. Lord! you are badly served here! (*Joséphine goes out the back.*) Thank goodness, they are gone. Here, Madame, take him.

(*He takes the child out of the cradle and gives him to Hortense, who goes into her room.*)

SCENE 9

THÉOPHILE, *alone, going to the buffet*

THÉOPHILE. And now that I have nothing more to do
. . . let me take care of myself. One always serves oneself the best. First, the table . . . and the tablecloth.
Look at me, a wet nurse! *(looking at the cradle)*

> *(To the tune of "La fête du village voisin")*
> These creatures that are so petite—
> What's not to love about a child?
> With their hearts so pure and mild,
> Children are so sweet.
> But one should not
> To little snots
> Give very many treats
> And if the boy
> Makes too much noise *(twice)*
> *(making a spanking gesture)*
> Smack, whack, smack, whack
> I'll calm him down just like that.
>
> Although I am only a novice
> My boss will take notice of me
> "No suitors!" I'll firmly decree,
> And he'll see that I'm never capricious.
> But if some ne'er-do-well
> Thought my figure was swell
> I'd suddenly stop being precious
> If he got close to me

And tried touching my knee *(twice)*
(making a punching gesture)
Smack, whack, smack, whack
I'll calm him down just like that.

(As soon as he sits at the table, he sees that the door to the left opens partially. He runs to take the baby that Hortense gives him and puts him back in his cradle.)

Well, that worked out well. And since the baby has eaten, I can do the same. Well, well, well . . . where is that wine . . . *(He rings.)* I wonder what that little Joséphine is doing? *(He rings again.)* Hey! Chambermaid . . . chambermaid!

SCENE 10

THÉOPHILE, *at the table,* JOSÉPHINE

JOSÉPHINE, *with a bottle in her hand.* What on earth?! You'd think the house was on fire!

THÉOPHILE, *with a full mouth.* A poor wet nurse that is dying of starvation, and that imbecile Dumont isn't bringing me my coffee!

JOSÉPHINE. I still can't get over this!

THÉOPHILE. That I got hired in this house? I told you, Joséphine.

JOSÉPHINE. But such shamelessness!

THÉOPHILE. What's the risk? Getting thrown out on the street? I was already out there, and also you don't know what it's like to be a cabinetmaker. It's almost like being an artist, with all the audacity and the farces . . . the audacious farces . . . it's my style. And, when you're in love with someone like I am . . .

JOSÉPHINE.   But what did you say to Madame to win her over?

THÉOPHILE.   That's my little secret.

JOSÉPHINE.   And this little baby? (*looking at him*) My God, he has just been nursed.

THÉOPHILE, *coldly.* I told you, Joséphine, love makes anything possible.

JOSÉPHINE.   But not that!

THÉOPHILE.   I'm telling you, yes. And I wanted to be in the house so I didn't lose sight of you, so I could monitor all the schemes of the boss. Now I'm here, at the table, but before I was underneath it . . . and I heard everything.

> (*To the tune of "Ma belle est la belle des belles"*)
> JOSÉPHINE.
> Everyone had a chance to listen.
> Though rich, with money saved,
> Monsieur is charming around women
> And always very well behaved.
> It doesn't cost that man a thing
> To give a girl a gift
> Nonetheless, the reason I'm listening
> Is that I have no other choices left.

THÉOPHILE. Is this all true?

(*Same tune*)
JOSÉPHINE.

You, sir, are jealous and like to sulk
And I never get flowers from you,
But if I get looks while out for my walk,
You get furious and stew.
(*Théophile gets up.*)
If I dance with the same man twice,
You become instantly bereft,
My dear, if I love you, to be precise,
It's that I have no other choices left.

THÉOPHILE, *forgetting himself.* Oh! Then I am the happiest of men.

SCENE 11

THE SAME; DUMONT, *bringing a pot of coffee, entering during those last words*

DUMONT. The happiest of men! What did I just hear?

THÉOPHILE. What! Who's there? That idiot Dumont! What's going on?

(*Théophile sits back at the table and Joséphine at the cradle.*)

DUMONT. Here is the coffee I brought you.

THÉOPHILE. That took quite some time, my dear. You had better show me some speedier service or I'll get you fired.

DUMONT, *aside*. We'll see about that.

THÉOPHILE.   All right, then . . . that's fine . . . you can go now!

DUMONT.   Does the wet nurse need anything else?

THÉOPHILE, *drinking*. No! Now that's good coffee.

DUMONT.   You don't need your room set up?

THÉOPHILE.   There's no need. I'm staying in Madame's room.

DUMONT.   Madame's room?

JOSÉPHINE.   In other words . . .

THÉOPHILE.   It's settled.

DUMONT, *aside*. So that's why he finds himself the happiest of men. I'm going to tell Monsieur about this. Goodbye, Nurse. Goodbye, my good woman!

SCENE 12

THÉOPHILE, JOSÉPHINE

THÉOPHILE, *getting up*. Where's he sneaking off to?

JOSÉPHINE.   I'm worried he heard something.

THÉOPHILE.   Nothing at all. That type is dumb by nature and born that way—not like artists or cabinetmakers, who are all witty.

JOSÉPHINE.   I'm worried you might be too full of wit, and therefore I am not letting you into Madame's room.

THÉOPHILE. Can it be possible? Jealousy? Oh, how happy you make me, Joséphine. I love jealous women. You could stab me right now and it still wouldn't make me any less happy. But don't worry. I'll ask for you to be there.

JOSÉPHINE. Well, I never!

THÉOPHILE. She won't be able to refuse me. A wet nurse is the mistress of the house. One is obliged to give in to all of her whims and desires. It's the beauty of the job. It's much better than being a porter like I wanted to be this morning.

JOSÉPHINE. But really . . . this can't go on.

THÉOPHILE. I know very well, Joséphine, that you cannot marry a wet nurse. I wouldn't want to either. But Monsieur Dalogny promised you a dowry of six thousand francs.

JOSÉPHINE. On the condition that I never marry.

THÉOPHILE. And what if, over the next few days, I take advantage of my position and arrange for you to have the dowry and the husband?

JOSÉPHINE. Really?

THÉOPHILE. On the condition that I be the husband . . . and that this lovely hand belong to me . . . and to me alone.

JOSÉPHINE, *lowering her eyes.* That goes without saying, Monsieur Théophile.

THÉOPHILE. And that turquoise ring . . . the one from Monsieur.

JOSÉPHINE. Do you think I care about that?

THÉOPHILE. I will take it.

JOSÉPHINE. Be quiet. It's him. Oh, how he looks lost in thought!

(Théophile sits back at the table and Joséphine at the cradle.)

SCENE 13

THÉOPHILE, JOSÉPHINE, DALOGNY

DALOGNY. What's this Dumont has just told me? He's claiming that this wet nurse . . . well, I will find out the truth! It's her! Come here, Madame Mitonneau . . . come here . . . so that I can look at you . . . well, well! Why are you lowering your eyes?

(Théophile stands up.)

THÉOPHILE. Naturally I do so when a man looks at my face.

DALOGNY. She is getting upset! Could Dumont be right? *(aloud)* Leave us, Joséphine . . . leave us.

JOSÉPHINE. What could this mean?

DALOGNY. Notify Lafleur and Petit-Jean to stand in the courtyard with two big clubs and to wait for my orders.

JOSÉPHINE. He's been outed, and there's no way to warn him. I'm going, sir . . .

(She leaves while making gestures to Théophile of hitting some-one with a club.)

SCENE 14

THÉOPHILE, DALOGNY

DALOGNY. Do you know, Madame Mitonneau, what I have just learned and what I am having difficulty believing?

THÉOPHILE. Is it something really terrible?

DALOGNY. You will be the judge of that. I've heard tell of trickery and disguises to gain admittance into my home. *(aside)* She's getting distraught.

THÉOPHILE. By God, is this possible? It's clearly robbers. I've always been scared of robbers, though sadly in our home there is nothing to steal. You need to give a statement . . . you need to warn the police commissioner . . .

(He makes as if to leave.)

DALOGNY, *holding him back*. Don't worry . . . it's not a robber.

THÉOPHILE. Well, what is it, then?

DALOGNY. A lover.

THÉOPHILE. A lover for me?

DALOGNY. Oh, no . . . good grief . . . a young man . . . a handsome young man . . . whom I do not know, but who has tried several times ineffectively to present himself here, and who, out of desperation, may have tried one final attempt that will nevertheless be unsuccessful.

THÉOPHILE. Well, how about that!

DALOGNY. My plan is to throw him out the window into my courtyard, where my men are waiting to club him.

THÉOPHILE. Excuse me?

DALOGNY. Unless he'd prefer to have his brains blown out . . . if you know what I mean.

THÉOPHILE. Why are you behaving this way with someone of the opposite sex? And to whom are you speaking, pray tell, sir?

DALOGNY, *quietly*. To you, Monsieur Melval . . . and to anyone who comes here for my wife.

THÉOPHILE, *calming down*. Good God! What a load of mudslinging! Me, Madame Mitonneau . . . mistaking me for a young man . . . for a handsome young man! You dare say it to my face!

DALOGNY. Be quiet, here comes my wife!

SCENE 15

HORTENSE, DALOGNY, THÉOPHILE

HORTENSE. What is this ruckus? What is going on here?

THÉOPHILE. Just that I can no longer stay here.

HORTENSE. But why?

DALOGNY. Well! Madame, you know better than anyone what is going on. I don't want to hear a single
word. You must not think that stockbrokers don't see
anything, and because I must speak clearly to the both
of you . . . there you are.

SCENE 16

THE SAME; JOSÉPHINE, *then* DUMONT

JOSÉPHINE, *entering through the back door and announcing.*
Monsieur Melval,[18] a young clerk, is here to talk with
you, sir, about an important matter.

DALOGNY, *shocked.* What? What could this mean? Monsieur Melval . . . is here?

JOSÉPHINE. In the sitting room.

HORTENSE. Well, go, sir, go . . . go ahead . . . or I will
welcome him.

DALOGNY, *approaching the door and looking.* Yes, a young
man. It's quite true. (*aside*) Oh, God! What have I
done? And where was my head? (*to Théophile*) Nurse
. . . my dear nurse, not a word about what I told you.

THÉOPHILE. What, sir? Mistaking me for . . .

---

[18] Different editions of this play introduce this character as M. de
Melval here. This typographical difference would have an impact on
the social class of this character, "de" signaling nobility.

DALOGNY. Pipe down! (*aside*) That alone would be
worth six thousand francs of mockery, and my wife
would make fun of me for the rest of her life.

THÉOPHILE, *crying*. After the way you've treated
me . . .

HORTENSE. What's this, now?

THÉOPHILE, *same*. I'm sure that I can't nurse today . . .
or tomorrow . . . or even the next day . . .

DALOGNY. Well! As you like . . . you don't have to do
it. We will keep you here with us.

JOSÉPHINE, *surprised*. Is this really possible?

DALOGNY. And to make you forget what just happened
. . . here. (*giving her a purse*) Here is a little bonus.

JOSÉPHINE, *shocked*. I can't believe it! They're apologizing and giving him money.

THÉOPHILE. Yes, my dear . . . because Monsieur is a
good master who recognizes his mistakes.

DALOGNY. It's not my fault, it's . . . (*noticing that Dumont has entered*) it's this imbecile Dumont's fault, who
just told me . . .

DUMONT. Who, sir?

DALOGNY. What on earth! When you eavesdrop, you
should listen better . . . or not get involved.

THÉOPHILE. The servants here are so awkward.

DALOGNY, *to Dumont*. If it happens again, I'll have to
fire you.

THÉOPHILE. It would be better if you just went ahead and did that.

DUMONT. Well, I never! The wet nurse . . . (*handing a letter to Dalogny*) Here's a letter that's just arrived from Poissy.

JOSÉPHINE and THÉOPHILE, *with fright*. From Poissy!

THÉOPHILE, *to Dalogny*. Are you going to read it? There's that man who is waiting for you.

HORTENSE. If it doesn't bother you, I will let him in.

DALOGNY. Oh, no, Madame. It's not worth it. Joséphine, give him my regrets. Tell him that right now, I cannot. I am indisposed . . . but maybe tonight.

HORTENSE. He can come for dinner.

DALOGNY. What?

HORTENSE. Since he has to talk to you about business, it's the least you can do for making him wait like this.

DALOGNY, *who during this time has unsealed the letter.* Well, well, all right, yes, go, Joséphine. (*looking at the letter with surprise*) Oh, my God!

JOSÉPHINE, *coming back.* What is it?

DALOGNY. It's none of your business . . . it's about Madame Mitonneau. Go where I told you.

JOSÉPHINE. Yes, sir.

(*She leaves.*)

SCENE 17

THÉOPHILE, DALOGNY, HORTENSE,
DUMONT, *at the table straightening up*

DALOGNY. It's a second letter from our farmer Gervault, whom you know.

THÉOPHILE. Certainly, a great man!

DUMONT. A good pal.

THÉOPHILE. Fit as a fiddle. And in such good health.

DALOGNY. He doesn't say the same about you, Madame Mitonneau.

THÉOPHILE. Excuse me?

DALOGNY, *reading.* "Sir, I wrote yesterday to let you
know that the wet nurse that I had reserved for your
son was very sick . . ."

HORTENSE. We knew that.

DALOGNY, *reading.* "I am writing you again, so as not
to keep you in suspense, for this morning, the poor
Madame Mitonneau has died."

ALL. She is dead!

THÉOPHILE, *aside.* What a blunder on her part!

DUMONT, *surprised.* You died this morning!

THÉOPHILE. Lord! This boy is dumb!

DALOGNY. It's possible. But what do you have to say
about it, Madame Mitonneau?

THÉOPHILE, *distressed*. I have to say, sir, that we are all mortals . . . and that certainly could have happened to me. I would have told you first . . . but the welcome that I received from Monsieur and Madame prevents me from pretending any longer . . . and because I must be honest, the truth is that I am not dead.

DALOGNY. Well that's helpful! Then who are you?

HORTENSE. How did you get here?

THÉOPHILE. I found my way! Because I do not know how to lie, and you saw how before, when you mentioned trickery and disguises, I got all flustered. But the desire to get hired into such a wonderful house, with such great masters about whom I had heard so much for such a long time . . .

HORTENSE. From whom?

THÉOPHILE. From . . . from Joséphine, your chambermaid and my relative.

DALOGNY. She's your relative?

THÉOPHILE. She's my very own sister, nothing more, nothing less. We're half sisters with the same mother.

DALOGNY. Is it possible?

THÉOPHILE. I am from our mother's first marriage. We are both ladies from Burgundy. I married a winemaker, who does nothing but make a baby every year. And so my sister wrote me often, "If you could be a wet nurse for Madame . . . you . . . who have such won-

derful milk . . ." It's true. I have wonderful milk . . .
and so that is how I got the idea to present myself here.

DALOGNY. Was Joséphine in on the plan?

THÉOPHILE. Truthfully she did not want to participate
at first . . . and I came despite her.

DALOGNY. That didn't stop her from playing her part
well. After this, watch out for seemingly innocent
young girls.

THÉOPHILE. As far as that's concerned, I know Monsieur has a certain interest . . . and I can sure tell you,
that whether you come from Poissy or Auxerre,[19] it
doesn't make a difference in terms of virtue or faith-
fulness. There's some of that in every department, and
Madame knows where my allegiances lie and what I
told her on that topic.

HORTENSE, *quickly.* Absolutely, absolutely. And I don't
see anything blameworthy here except the deception.

THÉOPHILE. There is no more deception.

DALOGNY. No doubt. But Joséphine is no less guilty,
and I would like her to explain herself.

(He goes to leave.)

THÉOPHILE, *holding him back.* No, no! I'm begging
you. Let me warn her, because, you see, that child
can't handle shocks and surprises. I know her, she will

---

[19] A region in northwest Burgundy.

be sick over it. I'm all worked up just from talking to you.

DALOGNY. Calm down, I will be reasonable. Besides, I will talk with her with no one around . . . a one-on-one.

THÉOPHILE, *aside.* Oh, my God! How to stop him? (*aloud*) Sir, I beg of you. (*aside*) I must cause a scene . . . there is no other way. (*aloud*) I am telling you I don't feel good. With all the emotion I've suffered today . . . I can't see . . . the milk is going to my head . . . hold me, I beg you. (*He falls into Dalogny's arms.*)

DALOGNY. Oh, dear, now she's sick . . . and in my arms of all things. Dumont, come help me out.

(*Dumont helps Dalogny place Théophile onto a chair. Théophile moves his feet and hands as if he were having a nervous fit.*)

> *Chorus*
> (*To the tune of "Serment"*)
> What torture! What a curse!
> I will certainly go insane.
> Both hell and the wet nurse
> Are here in our domain.

(*Hortense rings.*)

SCENE 18

THE SAME; JOSÉPHINE

JOSÉPHINE. What is wrong with you, Madame? What is going on?

HORTENSE. A horrible scene . . . your sister is ill.

JOSÉPHINE, *shocked.* My sister?

DALOGNY. Why, yes, of course, your sister.

JOSÉPHINE. I've never had one.

DALOGNY. Look at that confidence! It's useless to pretend.

HORTENSE. Everything is out in the open.

JOSÉPHINE. Who let it out?

DALOGNY. Madame Mitonneau.

JOSÉPHINE, *surprised.* She told you?

HORTENSE. She is more candid than you are. Don't just stand there not moving . . . go ahead . . . are you going to let her die? I'm going to loosen her corset.

JOSÉPHINE, *jumping in.* No, Madame, I won't stand for it.

HORTENSE. But there is no other way.

DALOGNY, *taking a pair of scissors.* Oh, my God, what airs! (*With one snip he cuts all the laces of the corset.*) Come on, Dumont, help me.

(*Dumont and Dalogny each pull on the sleeve of Théophile's jacket, which breaks into two and reveals a man's buttoned frock while the rest of his body, from the waist to the feet, stays covered by the skirt).*

ALL: Lord! I can't believe my eyes!

DUMONT: That's her sister?

DALOGNY. But that sister is a brother!

JOSÉPHINE, *hiding her face.* We are done for!

(Théophile, who has thrown off his skirts, tries to run away.)

DALOGNY, *running after him and bringing him back.* No, no, you will not leave, and I will finally learn who this scoundrel really is.

JOSÉPHINE. It's Théophile.

THÉOPHILE. A suitor who came for Joséphine.

DALOGNY. A seducer!

THÉOPHILE, *quickly.* No sir, on the contrary, I would call a seducer a married man who would slip a carnelian[20] or turquoise ring onto a young girl's finger . . . like this one, for example, this one here. But I am keeping it and will only give it to my fiancée if Monsieur allows it.

DALOGNY. Who, me?

THÉOPHILE. Yes sir, I know that you promised to give Joséphine a dowry of six thousand francs, if she was well behaved. I hope that you will forgive all the

---

[20] A reddish-brown semiprecious gemstone.

errors that love made me make. Who among us is not guilty of the same? No one. And if I were only to tell Madame . . .

DALOGNY.   It's fine . . . it's fine. No more explanation necessary. That's already enough. He can have the dowry.

THÉOPHILE.   And the lady?

JOSÉPHINE.   And a job as footman?

DALOGNY, *to Hortense.* Certainly, since he is ambitious he can ride behind your carriage. (*with emphasis*) His wife stays here.

THÉOPHILE.   Such generosity!

(*He salutes with his woman's bonnet, then, removing it, goes toward Joséphine.*)

DALOGNY.   You can see that I forgive him. (*aside, looking at Josephine*) But he will pay the price.

HORTENSE.   No more wet nurses. It's too much trouble.

DALOGNY.   No, Madame. You can nurse your firstborn.

THÉOPHILE.   And my wife will nurse the second. Because soon in our home we will say:

> (*To the tune of "Ave Maria"*)
> Sleep tight, baby, sleep tight
> I just hope and I pray
> That he will get his way
> All day and all night.

JOSÉPHINE, *to the audience.*
We've had one hope, and this is it
To entertain you, to delight.
So to those of you down in the pit,
Please don't say tonight:

"Sleep tight, baby," from out in the crowd
And if someone is dozing,
Wake them up, I'm proposing,
With a bravo—nice and loud!

ALL.
Sleep tight, baby, sleep tight . . . (*etc.*)

DELPHINE DE GIRARDIN

Letter 27

From *Parisian Letters*
by the Vicomte de Launay

Delphine de Girardin was a poet, playwright, and journalist. Her literary salon was frequented by the preeminent authors of her time. Her most-read works include Contes d'une vieille fille à ses neveux *(1832;* Tales from an Old Maid to her Nephews*),* La canne de Monsieur de Balzac *(1836;* The Cane of Monsieur de Balzac*), and* Il ne faut pas jouer avec la douleur *(1853;* One Should Not Play Around with Pain*). From 1836 to 1848, under the pseudonym Charles de Launay, she contributed weekly sketches of contemporary life to* La presse *(*The Press*), a daily newspaper published by her husband, Emile de Girardin. The collected columns were published under the title* Lettres parisiennes *(*Parisian Letters*) in 1843.*

---

30 November 1839

The sidewalks of Paris.—Foreigners.—The scientific community unsettled.

Wow! What a crowd! The sidewalks of Paris are teeming with people! One can hardly walk in a straight line. You have to step aside constantly to yield the way to a passerby, either a respectable or a threatening one.

There's the dignified old man in a puce-colored silk coat, accompanied by a servant wearing a redingote[1] that lets him pass for a friend.

There's the venerable elderly woman walking a frisky greyhound dressed in the latest fashion: a green velour jacket and a cherry-colored collar made of Moroccan leather.

There's the woman who, six months pregnant, is dragging herself along with difficulty.

There's the schoolmistress taking two charming little girls by the hand. She walks at a steady clip and takes on a serious and scolding air. Her enormous hat is rather tasteless and lacking style. The poor young woman has only one thought: how to hide the fact that she is young and especially the fact that she is pretty. She has often been reprimanded for this flaw, but those same critics are grateful for the efforts she has made to correct herself.

Those are examples of respectable passersby. The threatening ones are more numerous.

There's the delivery man carrying a wooden bed panel attached to hooks.

----

[1] A double-breasted outer garment, popular in the late eighteenth and early nineteenth centuries.

There's the florist whose basket is filled with shrubs. Be careful of her fresh rosebushes. They may have no roses, but they definitely have thorns.

There's the fishmonger, whose stall is set up with great symmetry. Her shiny eels—symbols of eternity—are placed in the center. The other fish (perch and whiting) are spread out in the shape of a fan and protrude most improperly over the edges. They invade the public space from every angle. Walk by quickly.

There is the washerwoman with an enormous square basket. All lacy mantelets,[2] quiver in fear!

There's the splendid coal merchant transporting a splendid sack of coal. Get ready to shudder, white satin hats!

There's the young locksmith who frolics with an iron bar on his shoulder. His curiosity is piqued, his imagination runs wild, for, it's worth noting, all locksmiths are witty. He thinks he sees one of his friends, a lovely young chambermaid. He turns around quickly to look at her, and the iron bar turns with him! . . . Look out!

There's the construction worker carrying oversized panes on his back and a bucket filled with paints in each hand. He can splash you with green or red: your choice.

There's the young grocery store clerk weighed down like a stagecoach.

---

[2] A short, sleeveless cape, mantle, or shawl.

He's carrying a sugarloaf, a barrel of anchovies, a jar of apricots soaked in brandy, salt, pepper, oil, and vinegar (he's a walking salad), a package of candles, etc., etc., and a carafe of lamp oil. He's dangerous: keep your distance. There's the butcher's dog whose collar has iron spikes.

There's the young pastry chef who is carrying on his head a sugary *entremets*,[3] a pretentious dish enjoyed by many diners.

There's the daydreaming child on his way to school, walking so slowly that he prevents you from moving. Or there's the happy schoolboy running home so quickly that he bumps into you.

At any rate, all the people you don't know from Adam are going on their merry way, not realizing that their way is also yours: they are walking to their destination without seeing you and inevitably stop you in your path.

I won't say, like Odry does in M. *Cagnard*,[4] that there are always more people in densely populated neighborhoods. I'll say instead that it's above all in

---

[3] A light dish served between two courses of a formal meal, usually after the roast and before dessert.

[4] Jacques Charles Odry was a comedic actor, playwright, and poet who often performed in popular plays. *M. Cagnard ou les conspirateurs* (*Mr. Cagnard; or, The Conspirators*) was a one-act show at the Théâtre des Variétés in 1831. The author and critic Théophile Gautier wrote in 1837 that "Odry a le nez taillé en bouchon de carafe" 'Odry has a nose shaped like a carafe's stopper,' after which Odry's nose became somewhat of a legend.

elegant neighborhoods that you see big crowds: the Rue de la Paix, the Rue de la Chaussée-d'Antin, the Rue Laffitte, the Rue du Bac, the Rue du Faubourg Saint-Honoré are now possibly even more bustling than the noisy Rue Neuve-des-Petits-Champs, the over-the-top Rue Saint-Honoré, and the hellish Rue de Richelieu.[5] I won't even mention the Rue Vivienne, where the passersby, hurried and jostled, walking in pairs along the sidewalks, seem to be dancing a sarabande[6] or a *pas de caractère*[7] in which all nations appear, that universal ballet one thousand times more lively than Musard's gallop.[8] This classic and yet fantastic street's reputation was established a long time ago.

---

[5] The first four streets in this list are in what are now the eighth and ninth arrondissements—areas that were just becoming fashionable at the time, where the nouveaux riches, the upwardly mobile bourgeoisie, lived. The latter three streets are in what are now the first and second arrondissements, which were more traditionally fashionable, associated with ancien régime aristocracy and old money.

[6] The sarabande originated in Latin America or Mexico and was danced by a double line of couples with castanets and lively music. It was considered disreputable in sixteenth-century Spain but spread to Italy and France in the seventeenth century and became popular in the French court, where it evolved into a slow processional dance.

[7] A classical ballet term referring to a character dance.

[8] Philippe Musard was a French composer who enjoyed enormous popularity during the 1830s and 1840s. He was credited with popularizing "light classical" music and and was best known for his "gallop" compositions. A gallop is a lively dance with a two-beat rhythm, orginally from Hungary, but eventually made popular in France.

Well, well, well! I found myself in this colossal whirl-wind for a week under the ghastly pretext of show-ing Paris to an English family. These twelve ladies—a mother, an aunt, and ten young girls—bestowed upon me the great honor of choosing me as their tour guide (read: servant). And there is not much to say about the boys, of whom there were only five, whose father took it upon himself to take them around. The first two mar-vels that the family asks to see upon arrival in Paris are the column at the Place Vendôme,[9] and the gem of the Comédie-Française, Mademoiselle Mars.[10] That's where all English families begin. So, we go to see the column. These women offer philosophical reflections on the great-ness and the fragility of everything human, to which I respond with clever thoughts that I will spare you here.

It's just a hop, skip, and a jump from the column to the obelisk,[11] that is, from the Place Vendôme, all we need to do is cross the Rue Castiglione and Rue de Rivoli and the Place Louis XV.[12] We admire the obelisk, and more

---

[9] The Vendome Column was completed in 1810 to celebrate Napo-leon's victory at Austerlitz.

[10] Mademoiselle Mars (Anne-Françoise-Hippolyte Boutet Salvetat) was a celebrated French actress.

[11] The Luxor Obelisk, the Egyptian obelisk situated at the center of today's Place de la Concorde.

[12] Place Louis XV is today's Place de la Concorde. Changes in the square's name reflect the vicissitudes of French history in postrevo-lutionary France. Originally named after Louis XV, the square was

philosophical reflections ensue, this time on earthly fri-
volities: on this needle of the desert that has come to be-
deck the noisiest of cities and where it now serves, they
say, as a lightning rod. We enter into the Tuileries garden
and everyone watches our charming procession go by.
Several well-dressed and impolite young men snootily
ogle these young women, who giggle at the pleasing demeanor of these charmers.

After an hour of walking, we race to the shops. We are
steered toward Mademoiselle Beaudrant's store.[13] The
mother, the aunt, and the two oldest girls are the only
ones permitted to visit this sanctuary. The rest of the
family waits for us by the door in their carriages. First,
they admire the rooms of this temple of taste, the high,
embroidered door curtains, those beautiful Japanese
vases filled with white feathers, bouquets in all colors.
These soon-to-be floral accessories are refreshed each
minute, for they only stay in their vase the time it takes
to be chosen. The ladies ask to try on a hat, so the Boulle

---

renamed Place de la Révolution in 1789 and became a public space
for the executions of the nobility. It is there that King Louis XVI was
guillotined in 1793. The square was renamed Place de la Concorde in
1795 as a gesture of reconciliation. After the restoration of the Bourbon
monarchy in 1814, the name was changed back to Place Louis XV, and
then again to Place de la Concorde after the Revolution of 1830. The
square has kept this name ever since.

[13] A famous Parisian hatmaker.

armoires are opened,[14] and the most charming hooded capes are presented. Four hats are ordered. One maternal hat in Indian velvet, decorated with branches of foliage in green velvet. For the aunt (who is still quite beautiful)— an adorable hooded cape in satin and gathered crepe fabric, velvet flowers, and Marabout feathers.[15] For each of the young girls—a delightful hooded cape in black velvet, decorated with a small black feather placed with an elegance that is impossible to describe.

We leave and go to meet up with the other family members, whom we find engaging in many forms of entertainment. All of the ambulant and open-air musicians of Paris are gathered around their carriages: all the Savoyards,[16] monkeys, and marmots are there. Jean Bonhomme,[17] the loveliest little monkey in town, pulls out all the stops trying to entertain our girls, whose merry laughter attracts a crowd and whose eminently

---

[14] André-Charles Boulle was a French cabinetmaker. Many of his pieces could be found in royal palaces such as the Tuileries and Fontainebleau.

[15] Feathers from the marabout bird, popular as adornment for women's hats and hairstyles of the period.

[16] A Savoyard is an inhabitant of or a person originally from the Savoie region. However, in popular terms, a Savoyard meant at the time a vulgar or coarse person. Savoyards worked in many different trades but were mainly known as chimney sweeps and street entertainers.

[17] This monkey is a recurring figure in popular culture. There is even a song entitled "Jean-bonhomme: Histoire d'un petit Savoyard" ("Jean Bonhomme: The Story of a Young Savoyard").

British beauty garners the admiration of the monkey's assistants. Jean Bonhomme plays the cymbals, sweeps the street, takes a passport out of his pocket and shows it to a police chief. He tries absolutely everything. The sight of this famous monkey makes us laugh too. I once saw a kind and witty friend sewing his little red suit. Indeed, one day I discovered this charitable woman by the fire, busily making Jean Bonhomme's little vest. She took pity on this wretched primate, an indigent whose seven-and-a-half-year-old Savoyard master did not have the means to dress him with dignity. Wishing to come to the rescue of such a respectable and ingenious monkey and to help him and his master make money, she nobly sacrificed an old shawl to make him an outfit. It was so generous. In any case, a woman of a certain age patiently sewing a vest for a monkey was quite funny.

They need another six hats. What color to choose? Blue? Pink? "I want an inane hat!" cried Miss Cecilia. First, we had a hard time understanding that "inane" meant "inflamed," as in flaming-red.[18] A flaming-red hat is a pleasant novelty, but six flaming-red hats in one family, well, that's a wildfire. In the end, white is cho-

---

[18] In French, the English girl says "un chapeau fou" (literally, a crazy hat) but she means instead "un chapeau feu" (a flaming-red or brightly colored hat). Here we take liberty with the translation to convey the joke.

sen. It's much more calming. Mrs. Goldberg, famous for inventing quilted hoods, is engaged for this order. Her chenille hats with velvet fringes are deemed charming. The group rushes to À la Péruvienne, on the Boulevard des Italiens, to choose mantelets. The most elegant ones are in white cashmere lined with cherry-red satin and embellished with fringe. The lovely aunt chooses one of these for herself.

For the girls, black capes lined with blue are chosen. At the same store, the mother is enticed by the exquisite headdresses. These are *demi-bonnets* adorned with a crown of flowers. What a stylish trick! What a clever way to prolong youth through fineries, to continue wearing garlands of flowers even into advanced age without any regrets. And why ever not? It is perfectly fitting to do so. Bold colors are only permitted for the very young. At sixty, wear pink. It's the most fitting shade. But wear it sensibly, with a high-necked dress and over a maternal bonnet.

We did a lot more shopping that I will tell you about later. But first I must tell you that, to satisfy the curiosity of our lovely friends from the British Isles, I brought them to the Théâtre-Français.[19] Mademoiselle Mars was performing in only one play that evening, a fact about

---

[19] Today, the Théâtre-Français is the Comédie-Française.

which the young English lasses complained bitterly. Miss Lucy said, "Mistress Blackway, my cousin, was in Paris only for six days last year, and she saw Mademoiselle Mars in two plays in the same evening." Such were their complaints, but imagine their surprise . . . Mademoiselle Mars plays the role of the duchess in *Les dehors trompeurs*![20] In that role, the great actress transforms herself. She is no longer the sweet and passionate heroine of a novel, a woman with stifled emotions who knows how to die of lovesickness in a ball gown, her heart broken, smiling with such grace, an angel of fortitude and goodness. Instead, she is a true high-society lady who's witty, insolent, happy, lively, teasing, and enviously cheerful. In the end, it is no longer Mademoiselle Mars, but rather Mademoiselle Contat. The British family is delighted. They thought this duchess was adorable, but were also a bit confused. They didn't expect this kind of admiration. Miss Lucy, not understanding anything anymore, kept saying, "Mistress Blackway, my cousin, explained that Mademoiselle Mars really made her cry!" "Mistress Blackway is right. When you see her in *Louise de Lingerolles*, you will indeed cry.[21] Meanwhile, my dears, listen

---

[20] A 1740 comedy by Louis de Boissy.

[21] A five-act play by Prosper Dinaux and Ernest Legouvé, performed at the Comédie-Française.

to *Les deux frères*[22] and watch Mademoiselle Doze, who is so lovely."[23] New applause from the audience for the young debutante, new delight in our theater box. Mademoiselle Doze acted brilliantly in the big scene of the second act; she was a screaming success. Monrose was perfect in the role of the old sailor.[24] It would have been impossible to be both more moving and more comical.

The scientific world is rocked by the appearance of a new phenomenon: a fake eel, a false lizard that everyone's fighting over.[25] Everyone is up in arms about the discovery of the *Proteus anguineus*.[26] This fish with paws—a lizard without eyes—lives in an uninhabitable habitat, in other words, the center of the earth. It can only be found in the subterranean river that penetrates the grottoes of Adelsberg. It is there that our traveler friend effortlessly fished one out last year. There is a significant stock of these creatures at the village grocer's, where you can buy them, alive or dead, at a very good price. I feel obligated to give these details to those

---

[22] An 1801 comedy by August von Kotzebue.
[23] Aimée Eléonore Léocadie Doze was a French actress.
[24] Claude-Louis-Séraphin Barizain, or Monrose, was a well-known actor at the Théâtre-Français.
[25] This non sequitur demonstrates the author's running commentary on contemporary fads and fashions in the *Parisian Letters*.
[26] An aquatic salamander.

naturalists who are searching for the *Proteus* right now all over the world. I will also add, to complete their annoying observations on the customs of this interesting lizard, that the *Proteus* lives wonderfully at the bottom of a night sack, without water, even when the jar holding it has broken. This observation was made by our friend, who, while in Venice, found the *Proteus anguineus* that he had brought with him from Adelsberg in perfect health and in the pocket of his coat. Apparently a German university has offered a good price for it. Question: Does the *Proteus* without eyes <u>see clearly</u>? Many naturalists have responded: he is myopic.

PAUL DE KOCK

A Grisette Party

From *Parisian Manners*

The term grisette *refers to a young, unmarried, working-class woman. A seamstress, an embroiderer, a hatmaker's assistant: this figure earned her name from the gray (*gris*) color of her inexpensive dress. The grisette was a pervasive figure in nineteenth-century popular literature and visual culture, and in novels that became canonical. For example, Fantine from Victor Hugo's* Les Misérables, *Ida Gruget from Balzac's* Ferragus, *and Rigolette from Eugène Sue's* Les mystères de Paris *(*The Mysteries of Paris*) are all a part of this lineage. Though the term is believed to date back to the late seventeenth century, by the early to mid nineteenth century, the grisette had become one of the most emblematic popular figures in French culture, often represented as being easygoing, hardworking, and flirtatious. Indeed, the grisette is usually depicted as the love interest of a university student, artist, or poet. A statue depicting the grisette can be found on the Boulevard Jules Ferry near the Canal St. Martin in Paris's eleventh arrondissement.*

Mademoiselle Adolphine, a young seamstress, was a pretty brunette: feisty, charming, even a bit cheeky. Her waistline was slender, her shape was curvy, her leg was dainty, her foot . . . well, her foot was not petite, but it was attractive and arched, which is better than a small, flat foot. At any rate, Mademoiselle Adolphine was very charming and never went out without turning a few heads—that doesn't mean anything, however, because ugly women do this sometimes too. There are so many men in Paris who don't know what to do with their time or with themselves and who, to put both to use, think they should follow and sidle up to every woman they encounter without a male companion. They follow one for her appearance and another for her waistline; this one for her leg and the other for her foot. And because nearly every woman has something pleasing about her, these men always find someone to follow and must be very tired by the end of the day.

Anyway, Mademoiselle Adolphine, at twenty-two years of age, with her beautiful black eyes, her turned-up nose, and her mischievous nature, must have been followed all the time, since men adore mischievousness and alluring looks. Why is that? My goodness, go ask them yourselves! As for me, I have my suspicions, but I can't tell them to you in this little story. I already got myself into hot water for calling one of my novels *The Cuckold!*[1] Besides, if I had to do it again, I can assure you that I would do the same thing, since I am used to not caring

---

[1] *Le cocu* (*The Cuckold*), published in 1831, is one of Paul de Kock's better-known novels. Like many of his works, it was deemed immoral by critics, in this case especially for its overtly sexual title.

too much about complaints and criticisms that don't come from the actual reading public.[2]

But all this is a digression from my lovely seamstress—let me get back to her. Adolphine had a reputation for being flirtatious. Some scandalmongers went so far as to say that she had lovers, because with those seductive eyes, a turned-up nose, and a nimble gait, it's almost unthinkable that a young woman would be well behaved.

This might be a truly unpleasant consequence for young ladies who resemble the portrait I have just sketched, but they have nothing to worry about. Everyone knows that appearances can be deceiving: a young person can be well behaved, even if they tease and laugh all the time, just as those who seem modest and shy, with downcast eyes, can still do silly things. I believe I even tried to prove this in one of my books with another unfortunate title: *The Virgin of Belleville*.[3] Just like the novel I spoke about earlier, this one also has a very moral objective, whereas many novels, even ones with irreproachable titles, are often very immoral. But there I go again,

---

[2] Here de Kock refers to the fact that he is simultaneously almost universally panned by literary critics and adored by his large reading public.
[3] A reference to de Kock's 1834 novel *La pucelle de Belleville*.

digressing from my grisette. I'll get back to her now, and this time I promise I won't stray.

For some time, a handsome young man named Édouard had been pursuing Mademoiselle Adolphine very zealously. Since Adolphine loved to laugh and chat, it was not hard to get to know her. And since Monsieur Édouard was proper, and his demeanor and appearance were distinguished, it was flattering to count him as a conquest. At any rate, for some while, the young man was welcomed into Adolphine's home.

When you've obtained permission to visit a grisette, it is quite natural to think that sooner or later you'll get permission to do something more, and that eventually you will achieve the ultimate victory. That's at least what Monsieur Édouard thought, and he was eager to proceed with Adolphine along those lines. But, to his great surprise, his attempts failed. First Adolphine laughed at his hemming and hawing; then she got angry when he got a little too friendly; and finally she told him in no uncertain terms, "If you want to keep coming here, you need to act properly." To which Édouard responded, "Is it improper to be in love? Why are you so pretty? Why do you make my head spin? I'll die if you're not mine!" and many more of those statements that are usually so effective with those women who are just looking to give in. But Adolphine just laughed again and said, "I am not convinced that you're in love with me. If you loved me, you would prove it by not acting this way. I only want to belong to my husband . . . yes, to my husband. Does that surprise you, just because I like to laugh and am a bit flirty, and I don't lower my eyes when I am looked at? That's just how it is. And this idea that you're going to die if I'm not yours . . . come on, Monsieur Édouard, that kind of talk is just as bad as those novels that are all about murders, dead bodies, and suicides. Those crime-filled tales disgust me, and that's all there is to it. Even though I'm just a simple grisette, I think I show my good taste by preferring cheerful, natural, and touching scenes over the horrible ones that make me shiver by day and give me nightmares at night!"

Édouard stayed silent; however, in order to be welcome at Adolphine's, he did have to promise to be well behaved. For that matter, men always make promises. They find that it doesn't commit them to anything.

So Édouard kept coming to visit Adolphine. Whenever she refused to kiss him, he sulked. After he had sulked for a while, Adolphine laughed. Sometimes for days at a time Édouard stopped coming to see the lovely seamstress, in hopes that he might forget her. But soon enough love guided him back to the grisette who smiled when she saw him, put out her hand as a sign of friendship, and gave him a little smack whenever he tried to kiss her again.

Nonetheless, carnival season arrived,[4] and so it became a time for pleasure, dancing, and fritters. People from all walks of life wanted to have some fun: even the lowliest civil servant threw parties, the rich merchant rivaled the nobles with his luxuries, members of bourgeois society engaged in traditional games and raffles, *portiers*[5] made crêpes in their lodges, and most grisettes went to masquerade parties.

Édouard offered to accompany Adolphine to these parties on many occasions, but Adolphine refused. She absolutely could not spend the night with him at a party—she worried about what could happen if she went home alone at night with a man who could not even behave himself during the day. Stung by Adolphine's rejection, Édouard went to parties without her and came to visit her less frequently.

Adolphine was heartsick and worried about losing Édouard's love. Just because you have a turned-up nose doesn't mean you're not sensitive. A sharp look can sometimes hide a loving heart.

---

[4] The period of celebration leading up to Lent.

[5] The *portier* is an employee of an apartment building who lives by the entrance and is in charge of keeping order in the building. In popular culture, the *portier* is seen as a figure who polices the comings and goings as well as behavior of the residents. The female version of this type, the *portière*, is also mentioned in this text.

One fine evening, Adolphine invited several of her girlfriends over. These ladies sewed a bit and talked a lot. "Everyone is throwing parties!" says Big Sophie.[6] "It's all the rage . . . In my building there is a floor polisher who had a masquerade party. I heard it was lots of fun! . . . There were people dressed as Spaniards and Turks . . . as shepherdesses and Robert-Macaire![7] . . . Apparently it was very fancy."

A tiny florist says, "I was invited to go to a high-society party in the home of a chair maker. You could decide whether or not to go in disguise. There was a supper, punch, ice cream, and games—both innocent and otherwise. We danced gallops[8] and ate warm brioche. In all the homes where I deliver my work, I see preparations for parties and feasts! Even my neighbor, who is a theater usher,[9] threw a nighttime party where they drank un-

---

[6] In the original French, the text switches between past and present tense.

[7] Robert Macaire was a popular stock character, an unscrupulous swindler. Created by the renowned actor Frédéric Lemaître in the 1820s, Macaire later appeared in a variety of works of popular culture. Best known among them are *Physiologie du Robert Macaire* (1842), written by Pierre-Joseph Rousseau and illustrated by Honoré Daumier, and a series of lithographs by Daumier that appeared in the widely read satirical journal *Le charivari* between 1836 and 1842.

[8] A gallop is a lively dance with a two-beat rhythm, orginally from Hungary, but eventually made popular in France.

[9] This type (*ouvreuse de loges*) frequently appeared in the popular culture of this period.

limited beer and even ate sausages at three in the morning! All the profits from those footstools they bring for the ladies at the theater converted into sausages! . . . Even my *portière* has parties! She makes nun's puff pastries with lard[10] on the stove in her lodge while her husband holds down the fort. What a feast!"

"So everyone in Paris is throwing parties!"

"Well then, my friends," says Adolphine, "why don't we do just as they do?"

"Us? . . . throw a party?" say the grisettes.

"We can if we want to . . ."

"Oh, we certainly want to! But how?"

"How about this: for the location, let me offer my place. I have a really nice room, and once we've taken out the furniture, it will be even bigger. I also have two spaces that we can use as the cloakroom and the dining room."

"Sounds good! And what else?"

"Then . . . well, there will be some costs for the lighting, the refreshments, and the supper, because we have to have supper, right?"

"Oh yes!" says Big Sophie. "I only dance so that I can eat!"

---

[10] "Nun's farts," or (more euphemistically) "nun's puffs," are desserts made from puff pastry dough that can be filled with cream.

"Well then, let's all pitch in, let's pool our funds, and if, as I hope, you trust me, I'll take care of all the details."

"Approved! Let's all pitch in!"

All the young women rummage around in their pockets. The result is a total of twenty-three francs, but with good friends, you know you will always have enough. They can count on pooling together about fifty francs, because the grisettes don't want their boyfriends to pay. It's a courtesy: the girls will throw a party for the boys.

With fifty francs, Adolphine anticipates that she will not be able to offer ice cream. But she promises to have a violin, a small flageolet,[11] cider and chestnuts in the evening, and a satisfying meal in the middle of the night. With everything arranged, they agree upon the date and start thinking about invitations. A young grisette skilled in penmanship sits at the table and writes down what Adolphine dictates to her:

"'You are invited to come dance and spend the whole night in the home of Mademoiselle Adolphine next Saturday. There will be a supper with a violin. Very sincerely yours'—Is that good, my dears?"

"Very good."

"Oh, wait; Foedora, write a postscript . . ."

"A post-what? What's that?"

---

[11] A woodwind instrument.

"Just keep writing. You put it at the bottom, below the signature: 'You must arrive by nine o'clock if you want to dance a gallop.'"

"Very good. That's the only way to force these fellows to come early."

"Now, Foedora, make as many of these letters as there are people we want to invite. I will just need to sign them. Okay, ladies, name the people you want to invite."

Each of the ladies names her boyfriend. In no time at all, the invitations are done, and the girls turn their thoughts to what they will wear for the party. It's the topic of conversation for the rest of the evening. At last, the grisettes go their separate ways, still discussing the pleasures to be enjoyed next Saturday.

Adolphine does not forget to send an invitation to Monsieur Édouard, and after that she thinks only about how to make her party splendid. Her friends give her thirty more francs. With the twenty-three francs she has already received, that totals fifty-three francs to work with. And she wants to add another fifteen francs of her own money if necessary, so that her party lacks nothing. The young lady calculates her costs. She wants to have two paper lanterns in the stairway, then, for her room, she will need to rent at least four oil lamps. For a party to be merry, it must first be well lit. Next, Adolphine creates the menu for her dinner. She needs a few pièces de résistance—poultry and pâté for the men and sweets for the ladies. Adolphine wants to satisfy everyone's tastes.

After having thought for a long time, this is how the young seamstress organizes the budget for her party:

Two lanterns	10 sous
Rental of four oil lamps and lamp oil	7 fr. 10 sous
Candles	10 sous
Sugar, cider, chestnuts, brioche	8 fr.
Pâté, poultry, sausage	16 fr.
Violin	6 fr.
Sugared pastry	9 fr.
Wine and coffee	15 fr.
Total	**62 fr. 10 sous**

Therefore, averaging a total of sixty-two francs and ten sous (grisettes never want to count by cents), Adolphine hopes to throw a delightful party. Until Saturday, the young lady plans out her outfit. She will dress as a Swiss farm girl. She makes the costume, tries it on, and says quietly to herself, "We will see what Monsieur Édouard does once he's seen me like this."

Finally, the big day arrives. She has to run errands and go rent the oil lamps, but first of all, she has to arrange a violin player. Adolphine goes to the address she was given. It's a rather dreadful house on the Rue des

Gravilliers.[12] Adolphine goes through an alley; she looks for a *portier*, but there isn't one. She goes up to the first floor, then to the second, telling herself, "You probably won't find a violin player on the first floor, especially a poor one who only gets six francs a night and who provides a flageolet."

Adolphine decides to knock on the third floor, because she hears music coming through the door. A young man with a violin in his hand opens the door for her. But he is a dandy, and inside his apartment Adolphine sees several young men, all dressed just as elegantly, each one holding an instrument.

The grisette is worried she's made a mistake. She stammers, "I would like to speak to Monsieur Dupont."

"Who on earth is Monsieur Dupont? I don't know anyone by that name, mademoiselle."

"Sir, he is a musician . . . a man who plays the violin at parties."

"Oh, wait a minute, mademoiselle, I think we actually do have an Orpheus,[13] a poor musician, in this building. I don't really know my neighbors yet, but if you want to go see, I think he's all the way upstairs."

---

[12] A street in a working-class neighborhood situated in what is now Paris's third arrondissement.

[13] A musician and poet in Greek mythology.

Adolphine offers her profuse thanks and rushes up the stairs. She arrives on the sixth floor and listens for the sound of the violin. But even though she strains her ears, she doesn't hear any music. All she hears are sighs and sobs. She decides nonetheless to knock on the door in front of her.

It opens, and what a sad sight appears before her eyes! In a scantily furnished room, a sick man is splayed out on a dreary little bed. Beside the bed are a tearful young woman and two children—an eight-year-old boy and a little girl no more than five—both pale and sorrowful, and seeming to share already in the burdens of their parents.

"My God!" says Adolphine. "I've made yet another mistake! I was searching for Monsieur Dupont, the violin player for parties."

"You've come to the right place," murmurs the weak voice of the person resting in the bed. "I am Dupont. Do you need my services?"

"Yes, sir, it is for a little party tonight at my place. I'm Adolphine, the seamstress, and I live on the Rue aux Ours[14] . . . but if you're sick . . ."

"Oh, yes, mademoiselle," answered the young woman, "my husband is very sick. It's because he's worked himself

---

[14] Another street situated in what is now Paris's third arrondissement.

to the bone trying to make money. Alas! My own poor father has been bedridden for quite some time . . . and then my poor little girl! We have suffered misfortunes for quite a while, and now my poor husband."

"Sadness has made my father sick," says the little boy. "Because tomorrow we have to sell all our furniture if we don't pay the landlord."

"Be quiet, Jules!" says the young mother. "Must you say such things?"

"These poor people!" says Adolphine, moved by the scene before her. "It would be barbaric to sell your belongings! Oh, these landlords are so cruel and so selfish. Do you owe much?"

"Eighty francs," murmurs the young woman, "and my poor husband is so sad that he hasn't the energy to work to earn such a sum!"

"And I'm not good enough on the flageolet. I can only play when accompanied by my dad," says the young boy.

Adolphine thinks, but says nothing. Suddenly, she races out of the room, saying only, "I will be right back."

She runs home, takes the seventy-two francs and fifty centimes intended for the party, and to that she adds all she possesses: eighty-five francs in total. Then she flies down the Rue des Gravilliers, runs up the six flights without catching her breath, arrives at the poor violin player's home, and places the money on a table near the bed, saying, "Here, pay your landlord, don't be sad any-more, and get better soon. We can always dance without music and have fun without eating."

The poor family can't thank her enough. Adolphine hugs the two children and takes off, saying, "Goodbye! I'll come back to see you."

The grisette returns home with a satisfied heart, feel-ing light as a feather. At first, she thinks only of the poor people she has just helped. But then she remembers the party she is supposed to throw that night. She begins to laugh and says to herself, "Too bad for those who come with an empty stomach! Oh, well, I'm still going to dress up as a Swiss girl. That won't cost me a thing!"

Adolphine gets dressed, straightens up her apartment, and waits for her guests with only one lit candle on her mantel. It doesn't illuminate the space well, but Adol-phine doesn't have a single penny left. That candle was her last one, and she makes it a habit never to buy any-thing on credit.

The clock strikes seven thirty. Adolphine's friends ar-rive and she can hear them calling in the stairway, "Adol-phine, light up the way! It's us! Why aren't the lanterns lit yet? It's very unpleasant to feel your way up four flights of stairs when you're dressed for a costume party."

Adolphine comes with her candle. The young girls en-ter her apartment and cry out, "My God! It's so dark in here! Why aren't your oil lamps set up yet and lit? What are you thinking, keeping us in the dark like this?"

Upon hearing this, Adolphine smiles and says, "Be patient, the oil lamps and lanterns are on their way." The young people invited by these ladies arrive shortly after. They seem a little surprised to see the party illuminated by just one lonely candle. The grisettes become angry and impatient and exclaim, "Adolphine, when on earth are they going to bring the oil lamps?"

"And the music, where is it?"

"Oh, it's coming," Adolphine replies. "While we're waiting, we can dance the *ronde*."[15]

"We didn't have a party just to dance the *ronde*," say the grisettes, "what will these gentlemen think of us?"

The young men don't say a word, but they smile in a mocking way. Édouard watches Adolphine and keeps silent. Now the kind seamstress is feeling embarrassed. Several of the ladies have already asked for a drink, and she has had to answer once again: the refreshments have not yet arrived.

Finally, with no light, music, or food in sight, the grisettes lose their patience and Big Sophie says to Adolphine, "My dear friend, you wanted to be in charge of

---

[15] A popular dance in which participants move in a circle or a line.

the party, but you didn't do a thing. What's going on? What did you use our money for?"

Adolphine blushes, hesitates, and finally says, "Friends, I didn't dare tell you . . . well, I lost my bag that had all my money in it. That's why I didn't have anything to pay for our party."

The young ladies seem concerned, the young men laugh, Édouard consoles Adolphine and reproaches her for not having asked him for help. Nonetheless, there is some whispering, and ultimately disappointment replaces cheerfulness. Some of the ladies even seem to question the story of the lost bag. Adolphine is beginning to grow angry when there is a knock at the door.

It is five well-dressed young men, each one holding an instrument: violins, bass, flageolet, all the makings of a lovely orchestra.

"Aha! Adolphine was just tricking us!" cry the young ladies. "Here is our music! I hope it's going to be wonderful."

"No, no! I told the truth," says Adolphine. "Sirs, there has obviously been some kind of mistake."

"No, mademoiselle," replies a young man that Adolphine now recognizes as the neighbor of the poor people she saved. "My friends and I are delighted to be here to provide you with dancing music, instead of my neighbor, that poor Dupont, who is in bed and to whom you generously gave all the money intended to pay for your party. We learned about your good deed from his son, and we hope you'll allow us to be your orchestra for the whole night."

His words reveal the truth. Everyone surrounds Adolphine to hug and kiss her. Now those who were upset tearfully ask for her forgiveness. In short, exhilaration and merriment abound. Quickly, the young men go out for candles and oil lamps. The party is soon glimmering. Then pastries and drinks are delivered. Finally, Édouard pays for the supper, and when Adolphine begins to protest, he says to her tenderly, "It will be our engagement feast."

AUGUSTE DE LACROIX

The Flâneur

From *The French Depicted by Themselves:*
A Moral Encyclopedia of the Nineteenth Century

The flâneur was a key urban type in the nineteenth-century French cultural imagination. A leisurely city wanderer, an artist, an astute reader and decipherer of the rapidly changing urban and social landscape, the flâneur was a focal point of much of the nineteenth-century urban literature on Paris, as well as of twentieth- and twenty-first-century scholarly commentary on it. As Priscilla Parkhurst Ferguson points out, this figure was "an emblematic representative of modernity and personification of contemporary urbanity" ("Flâneur" 22). Walter Benjamin, in The Arcades Project, *famously devotes an entire section to the rich archive of nineteenth-century flâneur writing. Though scholars have recently called attention to the importance of the female flâneuse,[1] the flâneur in the nineteenth century was usually a bourgeois male, someone who had time on his hands to wander the streets of Paris. He is first mentioned in an 1806 anonymous pamphlet about M. Bonhomme, a man of leisure who spends his days looking at urban spectacle, watching the crowds, visiting shops and cafés, etc. (Ferguson,* Paris as Revolution *82–84). In his early incarnations, the flâneur was associated chiefly with laziness and inactivity.*

As the nineteenth century progressed, the flâneur evolved into more complex character associated with artistic production. In the

---

[1] See D'Souza and McDonough, Kessler, Marcus, Nead, and Nesci.

1830s and '40s, the flâneur became linked with the figure of the writer, a keen observer who was capable of understanding and explaining the rapidly changing metropolis. This association reached its apex in the work of the poet Charles Baudelaire, for whom the flâneur was a quintessential representation of the modern poet, a privileged yet alienated interpreter of the city.[2] However, by the last decades of the nineteenth century, as the flâneur became a less culturally valued figure and a more democratic one, the connection between flânerie and writing diminished.

Do you know a term more appropriate to its idea, a more exclusively French word to express a perfectly French personification? The flâneur! An amiable type, a charming word, born one fine spring day from a happy ray of sunshine and a fresh breeze, on the lips of an artist, or a schoolchild or an urchin—those three great neological forces.

The flâneur is, without question, a native and a resident of an immense city—Paris, of course. In fact, there is only one city that can be the scene of his constant explorations. Only the flightiest and cleverest people on earth could have produced this kind of unwitting philosopher, who seems to exercise an innate ability to grasp

---

[2] We find the flâneur in numerous texts by Baudelaire, including "La foule" ("The Crowd") and other prose poems from *Le spleen de Paris* (1869; *Paris Spleen*), several poems in the "Tableaux parisiens" ("Parisian Panoramas") section of the 1861 edition of *Les fleurs du mal* (*The Flowers of Evil*), and his celebrated essay *Le peintre de la vie moderne* (1863; *The Painter of Modern Life*).

everything in one quick look and to analyze while walking by. The flâneur is an essentially French creature, and thereby generally different from other great men who might come from any other country, and especially different from the tourist who makes his observations in passing. The flâneur undoubtedly also likes movement, variety, and crowds, but he is not driven by an irresistible need for locomotion. He gladly delimits his territory, as long as he is able to nourish his soul daily. Thanks to his marvelous insight, he still knows how to harvest incredible riches from the depths of this massive field of observation where the vulgar individual only harvests from the surface.

As has already been made clear, the term *flâneur* must not be debased by using it to refer to those fake, more or less ridiculous versions of this estimable type, who walk all day out of dull and bored idleness. This would be an unheard-of usurpation, even in a century when aristocratic distinctions are within reach for those with only the most common ambitions! Our understanding of *flâneur* is limited to that small number of privileged men of leisure and wit who study the human heart in its natural habitat, as well as society in that great book of the world, open right under their noses. The observer at rest is only halfway an observer. The true observer is the flâneur, that man of subtle intelligence who is incessantly exploring everything (especially the human race), in all places, at all ages, and in all walks of life. He is a contemptuous philosopher who studies just as the peripaticians once held their discussions.[3]

The existence of the flâneur should not even be acknowledged outside of Paris. What is the flâneur in the provinces other than a pitiful dreamer with tired eyes and a dampened spirit from contemplating the same objects and who ends up not settling on any of them?

To the untrained eye, the flâneur cannot, at first glance, be distinguished from that particular species of bipedal human generally known by the name of gawker. However, there are huge differences that need to be pointed out. The flâneur is to the gawker what the gourmet is to the glutton, what Mademoiselle Mars[4] is to a mediocre actress, what Chateaubriand[5] is to a lowly copyeditor, or rather what La Bruyère[6] or Balzac is to a peasant from Auvergne or Limousin who just arrived in Paris yesterday. The gawker walks for the sake of walk-

---

[3] Peripaticians were disciples of Aristotle. The Greek word literally means "of walking" or "given to wandering." Allegedly, Aristotle was given to walking while lecturing. Curiously, the feminine form of this word in French, *péripatéticienne*, means "streetwalker, prostitute."

[4] The celebrated actress Anne-Françoise-Hippolyte Boutet Salvetat.

[5] François-René de Chateaubriand was a writer, diplomat, and politician and was a key figure in the French Romantic movement.

[6] Jean de La Bruyère, author of *Les Caractères* (1688; *The Characters*), was a French philosopher and moralist.

ing. He is entertained by everything, runs indiscriminately into everything, laughs for no apparent reason, and looks without seeing. Like a beetle, he goes about his life batting his wings against everything he comes across, colliding or smashing at any moment. He is a plaything of the wind that blows or of the urchin that walks by. With him in mind, wise sages have written, "He has eyes and will notice nothing; ears and will hear nothing." The expression "daydreaming" seems to have been invented with him in mind. He will effectively spend hours eyeing a flying swallow or a buzzing fly, without having the simplest thought or without any ulterior motive. The gawker doesn't think. He only perceives objects from the outside. There is no communication between his brain and his senses. For him, things only exist simply and superficially, without particular character or nuance. The human heart is a monolith whose hieroglyphs are in no way of interest to him. Philosophical deduction is unknown to him. To him, societies are just collections of men and monuments, a mere heap of rocks. A popular scene could be summed up for him by a certain number of insults and punches. He could be in a mine about to discover a lode of precious treasures and then turn around to follow a barking dog or a beating drum. He is the inventor of recreational fishing, of those ingenious pastimes like skipping stones to make concentric circles in the water. Between these two species of living organisms, there are all stages of creation, the distance that separates man from a polyp.

The bodily sheath of the flâneur is more or less the same as that of other animals known euphemistically as thinking and reasonable. Like these animals, he has a sufficiently nondescript and usually harmless face, except when one of his aimless walks is disturbed or when someone blocks his view of the acrobat he is admiring or interrupts the gossip he is listening to, in which case he shoots dirty looks and his usual mild manners turn ferocious. Otherwise, he dresses like everyone else and walks like you and me, although he trips much more often, despite the fact that he walks more slowly and takes his time to get a better look. Some—hypocrites and flâneurs in disguise—claim that the individuals we are attempting to describe here must necessarily see, with the eyes of the observer, distinguishing features that elude the untrained eye. They will tell you that a thorough examination will uncover a mocking keenness in their imperceptible smile and a prodigious insight in their expression. They will tell you . . . What do I know? That a certain posture, a certain wrinkle of the face, reveals a certain intellectual superiority. Here, the depth of thought, the power of logic, the perception of distant connections; there, the quick and subtle analytical mind.

Hallucinations of science; poetic alchemy for fanciful imaginations. Be wary of this mania imported from the novel into real life by those idealists of physiology; intellect does not influence the human face. I know men endowed with eminent faculties who smile stupidly, and I've seen people affected by moral cretinism whose expression shines with intelligence.

The flâneur is an essentially complex being. He does not have one specific taste—he has all the tastes. He understands everything. He is liable to experience every passion. He explains all eccentricities, and he always has an excuse at the ready for all weaknesses. He possesses an inevitably malleable nature, an artistic temperament. Therefore, he likes the arts like a constitutional monarch. He is a dilettante: painter, poet, antiquarian, bibliophile. Like a connoisseur, he enjoys an opera by Meyerbeer,[7] a painting by Ingres, an ode by Hugo. He sniffs out an Elzevir,[8] preys upon the street artists, and chases after the grisette. He admires Mademoiselle Rachel[9] and has

---

[7] Giacomo Liebmann Beer, or Meyerbeer, was a German-born opera composer who spent most of his career in Paris. He was one of the most successful stage composers of the nineteenth century.

[8] The House of Elzevir was a family of Dutch publishers, printers, and booksellers in the seventeenth and eighteenth centuries. The Elzevir editions were prized by bibliophiles.

[9] Mademoiselle Rachel (Elisa Félix) was one of the most celebrated French stage actresses of the nineteenth century.

a soft spot for Odry.[10] You will find him everywhere: on the promenade, at the Bouffes, at concerts, at sermons, at the Funambules, in salons, at dance halls, at the Boulevard de Gand, and in the Rue de la Grande-Truanderie.[11] He poses before pottery from ancient Susa,[12] stands in turn at the foot of Notre-Dame and by the stand of a used bookseller. He is curious, almost indiscreet. He is a man whose love of science can push him to cruelty and who, at times, takes as the subject of his experiments the very heart of his most intimate friend.

The flâneur is like all beautiful things. Like pretty women, he has no age . . . He can be between twenty-five and sixty years old, as long as he is in full possession of his intellectual and locomotive faculties. Since the flâneur is just as much in need of his legs as of his mind, when the former are lacking, he moves on to the state of observer. It is a different type of existence, a different

---

[10] Jacques Charles Odry was a comedic actor, playwright, and poet who often performed in popular theatrical works.

[11] Boulevard de Gand was the name of the Boulevard des Italiens during the Restoration. It was a popular site for flânerie. The Bouffes and the Funambules were popular theaters specializing in comedy and pantomime. Rue de la Grande-Truanderie is an old Parisian street located in the first arrondissement. The street's name likely comes from the word *truand*, meaning "pauper," "lazybones," or "beggar." Here it is likely a tongue-in-cheek reference to the flâneur's ostensible laziness.

[12] A collection of pottery from ancient Susa (in modern-day Iran) at the Louvre museum.

condition. His nature splits in two and weakens. It's the beginning of the end.

Paris belongs to the flâneur through the right of conquest and through birthright. Every day he crosses it in all directions. He scrutinizes all its depths, and he records in his mind the city's most obscure nooks. He sees everything on his own, and incessantly walks his sharp ears and eagle eyes around Paris. He misses nothing: he knows both today's and yesterday's news down to the smallest details. He knows what to believe and what to reject in the debates on correctional police as found in the *Gazette*.[13] More than the king's prosecutor or the police chief, he knows where and how the bloody drama (to adopt the public prosecutor's vocabulary) got started—the drama that has horrified society and that calls for a great and salutary example from the law. I should say he knows many other things! He knows how laws are drafted and executed. He knows the price of a vote, the secret of the improvisations of one orator, and the price another paid for his last speech. He will tell you where the most beautiful art gallery can be found as well as the richest collection of antiques and autographs; which amateur owns the only existing self-portrait of Raphael;

---

[13] A reference to the *Gazette des tribunaux: Journal de jurisprudence et des débats judiciaires* (*Court Gazette: Journal of Jurisprudence and Judiciary Debates*), a publication that reported on the latest crimes and legal cases.

which library has the rarest Alde and Elzevir editions.[14]
He also knows which happy Parisian jockey owns the
number one thoroughbred and the best trotter; which theater director boasts the sweetest soubrette,[15] and which
ballet company has the dancer with the roundest leg.
What am I saying? To him we owe the most precious dis-
coveries and the most marvelous inventions. Who reveals
the fresh new talent to us every day? Who most recently
discovered Mademoiselle Rachel lost amid the mediocrity
of the Gymnase?[16] A director-flâneur. Who discovered galvanism?[17] A physicist-flâneur on his balcony accompanied
by a frog. To whom do we owe the knowledge of the laws
of electricity, of attraction, of unit weight? To scholars, naturalists, and mathematicians, all playing hooky. Who invented the compass? A sailor on duty, playing with a piece
of metal. Who invented gunpowder? A monk strolling
along the crumbling walls of an old convent. Art, science,
and literature owe more or less all their daily progress to

---

[14] Edward Alde (or Allde) was an English printer active during the
Elizabethan and Jacobean eras, known for significant titles of English
Renaissance drama, including early editions of plays by Shakespeare.

[15] In theater, a comic type; a lighthearted, mischievous, and flirtatious young girl, often a chambermaid.

[16] A reference to the Théâtre du Gymnase (opened in 1820), a venue
for vaudevilles and other popular plays.

[17] Named for the Italian physicist Luigi Galvani, who discovered the
phenomenon in 1780, galvanism refers to electric current generated by
chemical action, particularly within biological organisms.

a flâneur. They stem from him and converge on him. He is the center and the social pivot. He has done more for philosophy and the study of the human soul than the most beautiful books and the most learned theories.

It has been noted that lazy people are also often witty. Indeed, it goes without saying that one must have many resources to fight boredom so as to live by one's own means, as the hibernating woodchuck lives off his own substance. This observation is particularly true in regard to the flâneur. But first and foremost, the terms must be agreed upon. For those for whom laziness means the absence of sustained activity, of any kind of regular work and of immediate usefulness, the flâneur is without a doubt eminently lazy. It must nevertheless be noted that the most occupied man is not the busiest man, and that work is not always perceptible to the naked eye. It is true that the flâneur produces very little, but he amasses quite a bit. Just let him reach the ripe old age of memories and meditation, that period of life similar to the moment of digesting learned ideas, when everything is classified and organized in one's brain as a result of the deep calm of the imagination and the senses. Let him reach the moment of retirement, in other words, of rheumatisms, ophthalmia, and hearing loss, and you will see this ostensibly idle and futile life taken up in the form of novels of manners and of philosophical works. When a book appears full of high philosophy and ingenious insights, it can be surprising to learn that it is written by a member of the elite, perhaps even by a young man you would disdainfully group among those idlers whose face is everywhere and whose mind is nowhere. Do you believe that the world is best understood in solitude, and that the human heart is a book one studies by the fireside? Without wishing to pry, I would very much like to ask the ingenious author of the *Physiologie du mariage*[18] which sources he mined for his profound understanding of the most inexplicable mysteries of feminine nature. There are certain flâneurs whom you disdain, who can tell you more about this topic than all the scholars and moralists combined. The one exception is the positivist sciences, where learning from tradition is necessary. For those sciences you need obsessive homebodies with sound intellects. But beyond that, the flâneur has a solid grasp on arts and letters. How many distinguished men began as obscure flâneurs! Who isn't aware of the strolling habits of the most powerful of the Chamber speakers?[19] Who doesn't

------

[18] *La physiologie du mariage* (*Physiology of Marriage*), by Balzac, was published in 1829 and is considered a precursor to the genre of *physiologies*.

[19] Created by the Charter of 1814, the Chamber of Deputies was a lower house of the French Parliament, elected by census suffrage (in which individual votes are weighed according to the voter's rank and status). The Chamber of Deputies was charged with discussing the laws and voting on taxes.

know the personality and artistic tastes of that little journalist whom the July Revolution suddenly turned into a
great minister, that most talented juggler of words, that
wittiest and most prolific chatterbox of the tribune?[20]
Ask those two men which treatise, Aristotle's *Rhetoric* or
Cicero's *Orator*, was delivered to them by the electronic
threads that are mysteriously connected to each one of
the fibers of the human heart.

But it is above all to literature that the elite flâneur
belongs. Here names just flow from my pen. Flânerie
is what defines a true man of letters. Talent exists in
this species merely as a consequence. The instinct of
flânerie is the primary cause. With some light varia-
tions, one might say: You are a man of letters because
you're a flâneur. Any objection would be an absurdity
proven by experience. Would you understand a professional writer, that is to say, a man whose main job it is to
depict customs and passions, who was not possessed by
a secret penchant for observing, comparing, analyzing,
seeing with his eyes, surprising nature in the act, so to
speak? Thus examples abound. The so-called hermit of

---

[20] A reference to Adolphe Thiers, a statesman during the July Monarchy who began his career as a journalist for the newspaper *Le constitu-
tionnel* (*The Constitutional*).

the Chaussée d'Antin[21] is an experienced flâneur who has
not yet been able to renounce the ways of his youth. The
author of the *Tableau de Paris* must have strolled quite a
bit.[22] What greater flâneur is there than La Fontaine?[23]
Rousseau strolled for two thirds of his life and spent
the rest recounting the very unedifying flâneries of his
youth.[24] As everyone knows, Racine studied the human heart backstage at the Comédie Française, which
means, incidentally, that his Greek and Roman heroines
undoubtedly have a French demeanor.[25] What about
Bernardin de Saint-Pierre, who, after having strolled
in both hemispheres, spent his entire day rhapsodizing
in front of a strawberry bush loaded with microscopic
insects and who, before the towers of the cathedral of
Rouen, admired only the swallows fluttering above his

---

[21] *L'hermite de la Chaussée d'Antin, ou l'observation sur les mœurs et les
usages français au commencement du XIXe siècle* (*The Hermit of the Chaussée
d'Antin; or, Observations of French Mores and Customs in the Early Nineteenth Century*) was a series of satirical sketches of Parisian life by
Étienne de Jouy (Victor-Joseph Étienne). The sketches were first published in weekly installments in *La gazette de France* (*The Gazette of
France*) from 1811 to 1814 and were later collected in volume form.

[22] Louis-Sébastien Mercier's sketches of Parisian life in *Tableau de
Paris* (1781–1788; *Panorama of Paris*) are considered a precursor to the
literature of urban observation of the 1830s and 1840s.

[23] Jean de La Fontaine was a seventeenth-century French writer particularly well known for his fables.

[24] A reference to Rousseau's *Rêveries du promeneur solitaire* (1776–1778;
The Reveries of a Solitary Walker).

[25] Jean Racine was a seventeenth-century French playwright.

head?[26] If the tourist is anything other than a traveling flâneur, then, I ask you, in what category does the author of *Atala* and *René* belong?[27] And what else but an eternal flâneries were those poetic peregrinations on the shores of the ocean, on the banks of the Ohio or the Mississippi, through the green savannahs of Louisiana or under the murmuring forests of Kentucky? Where would we be today if a vague instinct for flânerie had not taken Chateaubriand, that Christian bard, near the ruins of Jerusalem or among the warring tribes of the Natchez to an old savage, poet, and storyteller who resembled him?[28] Who among us has not come across, on more than one occasion, the wise linguist, in mid-flânerie on the Quai des Augustins or on the Boulevard du Temple, the elegant writer whose delicate good-heartedness could have legitimately come from La Fontaine? Who among us does not know of his passion for Polichinelle, his admiration for Debureau, and his regular attendance in the boxes of the Funambules?[29]

---

[26] Bernardin de Saint-Pierre was the author of a widely popular novel, *Paul et Virginie* (1788; *Paul and Virginia*).

[27] *Atala* (1801) and *René* (1802) are novels by Chateaubriand.

[28] This sentence contains several references to *Atala* and *René*.

[29] Jean-Gaspard Deburau (misspelled in the original text) was a French-Bohemian mime who spent most of his career performing at the Théâtre des Funambules. He is depicted in Marcel Carné's film *Les enfants du paradis* (*Children of Paradise*).

To that end, the author of *Trilby*[30] himself told me an anecdote that proves that the taste for flânerie is no more incompatible with the elevation of the mind than with the gravity necessary for important duties.

When Monsieur Français de Nantes[31] was named administrative director, he hired a great number of men of letters who enjoyed the leisure that a comfortable position afforded them, so that they could successfully devote themselves to their creative pursuits. Among the privileged writers and those most worthy of this honor bestowed upon their talents was the pure and graceful poet who later wrote *Fragoletta* and *La vallée aux loups*.[32] Monsieur Français de Nantes had a particular esteem and affection for this writer. He made a point of offering him a job that required little work. The lucky sinecurist[33] could luxuriate and dream at his leisure in his bureaucratic chair while waiting for something better to come

---

[30] *Trilby, ou le lutin d'Argail, nouvelle écossaisse* (1822; *Trilby; or, the Goblin of Argail: A Scottish Tale*) is a novella by the Romantic writer Charles Nodier.

[31] Antoine Français de Nantes was a French politician active during the French Revolution and under Napoleon I. He was well known for employing artists and writers as well as aristocrats dispossessed by the Revolution.

[32] Henri de Latouche's novel *Fragoletta, ou Naples et Paris en 1799* (*Fragoletta; or, Naples and Paris in 1799*) was published in 1829. *La vallée aux loups* (1833; *Valley of the Wolves*) is his volume of essays.

[33] This nineteenth-century neologism—in French, *sinécuriste*—refers to a beneficiary of a sinecure, a job that requires little work for substantial pay.

along. Regular attendance was the only requirement. For three months, everything went well in the best and most pleasant of administrations. At that time, the punctual bureaucrat seemed to lose, little by little, his feeling of obligation, that religion of virtuous women and irreproachable employees. More than once, his surprised colleagues exchanged ambiguous smiles and not-at-all ambiguous words at the sight of the humble hat hook without the bureaucrat's habitual fedora and the unfortunate chair of soft mahogany consistently left empty. The scandal grew and grew; the paper-pushers complained. The wind, or another busybody of the same genre, let the news slip under the door of the director's office. One day, the tardy employee was standing, his head lowered with a contrite look, before his boss. The latter, uncharacteristically, had his brow furrowed and a severe look about him.

"I hear, sir," he said, "that you are not fulfilling the one requirement I allowed myself to impose upon you. Are your duties so arduous? Should I withdraw something from your daily work for the administration? Did I make the position too difficult?" All this was said in a tone of friendly reproach that deeply concerned the guilty party.

"Believe me, sir, that my gratitude . . ."

"How about, instead of justifying yourself to me, you go back, if not to your duties, then at least to your office, as we had agreed upon?"

"All right," responded the employee, visibly bothered, after a moment of hesitation and trying to make an effort, "I see that I must move out."

"Excuse me, sir," replied Monsieur de Nantes swiftly, mistaking the intention expressed by these words, "is this your gesture of gratitude?"

"Excuse me, sir, I only meant that I will be forced to leave the residence I took a few days ago."

"Ah! I understand, you live in the country and that is what causes your lateness and frequent absences."

"I must confess, sir, that I live in Paris."

"Well, then, please do me the honor of explaining this enigma to me."

"Oh, well, that's exactly the problem . . . I would never dare . . ."

"I see what this is," said Monsieur de Nantes, smiling maliciously, "you are experiencing some great passion, Mr. Poet, under the power of a jealous mistress, possibly a demanding one, who tyrannizes you and keeps you on a tight leash."

"Alas, sir, I do not have any mistress at present except for poetry, and no other passion except for fame. But I have a weakness . . . one that makes me blush . . ."

"Well, what is it? Could it be wine? Gambling?"

"You will never guess it, sir," said the young man suddenly with a resolute air. "I may as well just tell you.

Please know that I live in the Marais, and to get here I have to walk along the entire length of the Boulevard du Temple, and it is always so lively, so loud, so packed with people and curiosities—teeth pullers, disappearing acts, jugglers, bear tamers, mermaids, children with two heads, giants, and crocodiles—that I'm tempted at every step."

"Oh, sir," interrupted the general director in a disdainful tone, "I would never have thought that a man like you could be interested in such things. It is surely not for that, I am afraid to tell you, that I took it upon myself to create a sinecure for you at the expense of the State. In doing so, sir, you had better believe that I had thought that the pastimes of a man whose talent I esteem would not be lost to art, nor, I should add, to such nonsense."

"I confess, Monsieur, that trifles in general, and insignificant trifles in particular, often carry for me a particularly irresistible charm. Polichinelle himself . . ."[34]

"What! You like Polichinelle?"

"Passionately."

"And you like to laugh at those kinds of buffoonery and tricks?"

"Every day, for at least an hour."

---

[34] Polichinelle is a stock character originating in the commedia dell'arte.

"How strange," replied M. de Nantes seriously. "I've never run into you there."

I could cite many more examples, if I weren't worried about overindulging this way of reasoning. Men of letters and artists could provide us with a profusion of these sorts of proofs by induction. Let's just remind ourselves here that Monsieur de Chateaubriand, who knows his stuff when it comes to geniuses, defined poets in the following way: sublime children.[35]

In fact, this simplicity of character, this apparent good nature that makes it so that one becomes interested in the smallest things and not afraid to penetrate life's vulgarities, is almost always the sign of eminent merit. True superiority does not degrade itself when it lets itself be seen and touched. It makes itself known and popularized through free access and casualness. Only dwarfs and those with deformities feel the need to wrap themselves in a cape and climb on stilts. Myopic minds take pity on people, wise and strong, who play with small children and try very hard to examine futile things. This divergence of opinion and behavior between these two classes of men can most naturally be explained by the infirmity

---

[35] "Enfant sublime" is a phrase that Chateaubriand allegedly used in reference to Victor Hugo when he was a young poet. There are scholarly debates as to whether Chateaubriand actually ever said this (Robb 565n50).

of the former. Some stop at the surface, others dive in deep: that's the secret of this difference. Under the first layer of everything there are undiscovered connections, unknown insights, a whole new world of ideas, reflections, and sentiments that awaken and spring up all of a sudden under the expert watch of the observer, like a hidden source under the probe of geology. For the vulgar person, the child who babbles, cries, or plays is just an incomplete being, the weakest and the least reasonable of all. For the physiologist,[36] he is a king of creation trying his hand at life, a man with instincts, passions, and native faculties which reveal themselves and hint at his future destiny. The man of the people, that abrupt nature whose primitive traits have not been erased by the social pressures; a civilized man, a living enigma, whose every action, every word is a lie and often a trap; a woman, that elusive chimera who does not know herself, who faints as soon as you figure her out and kills those who cannot explain her; society, that inextricable labyrinth; in the end, the world, that great enigma, bigger than all the others, whose word is kept in God's lap: everything exists, lives, moves, and poses for the observer. Yet, as I have said, what else is the flâneur if not an observer in

---

[36] An author of *physiologies* such as the ones included in this volume (see Introduction).

action, an observer in his most elevated and eminently useful expression?

A woman asks us if the flâneur is in love. —A profound appreciation for everything beautiful is the defining feature of his character. —"Consistently?" —Alas, go ask the philosopher which abyss exists in man's soul. Go ask the poet if his love is constant. Go ask the traveler which irresistible instinct inspires him to search endlessly for new sights, warmer climates, and greener pastures. Go ask the sailor if his heart is not as vast as the ocean and as changing as its waves, to how many shores he has moored his ship and cast his affections, if he has found any lands as beautiful to his eyes as the ones that he hasn't yet visited, and any relationships able to resist the vagaries of the elements and the gusts of passions. Let us not hold the Supreme Wise One accountable for the faculties distributed to each of his creatures, nor the flâneur for the inherent imperfections in his exceptional organization. Let us not ask the swallow why it flutters, the stream why it winds as it flows, the flâneur why he strolls. Today, so many others enjoy denigrating this friendly and fickle national type who continues to recede more and more. Let us leave to the blind the sad privilege of disdaining light, to the deaf to deny the harmony of sound, to the fools what they do not understand. Who among us does not feel in their heart a secret

sympathy for the good, easy, inoffensive, and witty being we call the flâneur? Who among us, after examining
their conscience, would dare to proclaim themselves so
pure of the sin of flânerie so as to throw the first stone at
the flâneur? Who are you, after all, you who read these
words? And who am I, who write them?

A flâneur.

The Proper Woman

From *The French Depicted by Themselves: A Moral Encyclopedia of the Nineteenth Century*

This piece, written in 1840, first appeared as part of The French Depicted by Themselves, *and then again in 1842 as part of a short novel,* Autre étude de femme *(Another Study of Woman). The title refers to a feminine type that emerged in the 1830s. The expression "comme il faut" means "respectable" or "proper." While Balzac is more commonly known for his novels and novellas grouped under the title* La comédie humaine *(The Human Comedy), at the time he participated in more commercial forms of writing; he contributed to several multiauthor works of panoramic literature and wrote a number of physiologies.*

One fine day, you're strolling through Paris. It's past two but not yet five in the afternoon. You see a woman walking toward you. The first glance that you cast at her is like the preface of a beautiful book: it lets you foresee many fine and elegant things. Like a botanist herborizing over mountains and valleys, you have finally found a rare flower amid all the Parisian vulgarity.

She is accompanied by two distinguished-looking gentlemen, at least one of whom is wearing a medal, or else a casually dressed servant is following her at a

distance. She wears neither dazzling colors, nor lace stockings, nor an elaborate belt buckle, nor ruffled pantaloons overflowing around her ankles. You will note that on her feet she wears either a high, lace-up linen boot (with the most exquisite cotton stockings or with gray silk stockings) or ankle boots of the utmost simplicity. You will also note the fabric of her dress, rather pleasant and inexpensive. The cut of the dress surprises more than one bourgeois woman: it almost always has a fitted coat attached with bows and decorated with a charming plait or an invisible thread. The stranger has a particular way of wrapping herself in a shawl or a mantle. Had a bourgeois woman worn such clothing she would look like a tortoise. But the proper woman manages to reveal her beautiful shape just as she conceals it. How does she do it? That's her closely kept secret, even if it's not protected by a patent.

Artists, poets, lovers—all you who worship ideal beauty, that elusive rose of the genius—go out and stroll and admire this flower whose beauty is so well concealed, so well revealed! The coquette walks with a certain concentric and harmonious movement that makes her smooth or dangerous figure quiver under the fabric of her dress, like a snake in the rippling green grass at noon. Is it to an angel or a devil that she owes this graceful undulation that materializes under her black silk cloak, agitates its lace trimmings, spreads ethereal balm around her, and that I would gladly call the breeze of the Parisienne? You will recognize on her arm, on her waist, and around her neck, the most carefully studied folds that cover the most wayward of fabrics that remind you of the ancient Mnemosyne.[1] Ah! How well she understands the nature of her gait! Look at how, when she walks, her dress molds around her legs with such precision that, for passersby, she provokes admiration mixed with desire, but a desire restrained by deep respect. When an Englishwoman attempts this way of walking, she looks like a soldier rushing forward to attack a fortress. The gift of walking belongs to the Parisienne! So it is to her that the municipal authorities owe the sidewalk pavement.

Your stranger does not collide with anyone. To get through a crowd, she waits with proud modesty until others make way for her. The particular distinction of well-bred women is revealed in the way they cross their shawls or their mantles on their bosom. When she walks, she looks dignified and serene, like Raphael's paintings

---

[1] The personification of memory in Greek mythology.

of the Madonna.[2] Her posture, at once calm and disdainful, makes the most insolent of dandies cede the way. Her hat, of the most remarkable simplicity, is trimmed with fresh ribbons. Perhaps there are some flowers as well, but the most capable of these women wears only bows. Feathers demand a carriage, flowers attract too much attention. Underneath the hat, you find the fresh and well-rested face of a woman, sure of herself without being smug, who looks at nothing and sees everything, whose vanity, inured by continuous satisfaction, spreads an expression of indifference across her face that piques your curiosity. She knows that she is being studied. She knows that almost everyone, even women, turn to look at her. And so she weaves throughout Paris like a gossamer: white and pure.

This beautiful specimen is fond of the warmest latitudes and the most appropriate longitudes of Paris. You will find her between the 20th and the 110th arcade of the Rue de Rivoli;[3] on the boulevards from the ardent equator of the Passage des Panoramas,[4] where the prod-

---

[2] Raffaello Sanzio da Urbino (Raphael) was an Italian painter and architect of the High Renaissance.

[3] A fashionable and recently constructed street that featured shopping arcades.

[4] A reference to the Passage des Panoramas, a popular shopping arcade, where one could purchase luxury items imported from India (such as cashmere shawls).

ucts from India flourish, where the hottest creations of
the fashion industry blossom, all the way to the cape
of the Madeleine;[5] or in the least mud-sullied regions of
the bourgeoisie; between the numbers 30 and 150 on the
Rue du Faubourg-Saint-Honoré. In the winter, she enjoys
herself on the Terrace des Feuillants[6] but not at all on the
sidewalk that goes along it. Depending on the weather,
she floats along the Champs-Élysées, which is flanked
by the Place Louis XV to the east, the avenue Marigny
to the west, a roadway to the south, and to the north
by the gardens of the faubourg Saint-Honoré. Never will
you meet this beautiful variety of woman in the north-
ernly regions of the Rue Saint-Denis, never in the Kamts-
chatka[7] of the narrow, muddy, commercial streets; and
never anywhere in bad weather. These flowers of Paris
bloom in the morning, perfume the promenades, and after five in the afternoon, they close like morning glories.

The women you will see later on in the day look a bit
like the ones just described, and indeed, they do try to

---

[5] Napoleon I ordered the Madeleine constructed as a monument
commemorating the glory of his army. Built in the form of a Roman
temple, it was turned into a church after the restoration of the Bourbon
monarchy. The interior was completed between 1828 and 1842.

[6] A popular place to walk in the Jardin des Tuileries.

[7] By naming a peninsula in the far east of Russia, Balzac evokes parts
of Paris located far away from the city center; in other words, the edge
of civilization.

imitate the proper woman. But these are not-so-proper women,[8] whereas your beautiful stranger, your daytime Beatrice,[9] is a proper woman. It is not easy for foreigners to recognize the differences by which experienced observers distinguish between them, because women are such good actresses! But these differences are blatantly obvious to Parisians: badly fastened hooks, strings that expose the mesh through an opening in the back of a dress, worn leather shoes, used hat ribbons, a too-puffy dress, a too-tight skirt. You will notice a certain effort in the way she intentionally lowers her eyelids. There is something conventional about this look.

As for the bourgeois woman, it's impossible to confuse her with the proper woman. Her shortcomings, in fact, bring out the charm that emanates from your lovely stranger. The bourgeois woman is busy; she goes

----

[8] In the French original, the proper woman (*la femme comme il faut*) is contrasted with the improper woman (*la femme comme il en faut*), one who is not respectable or marriageable and cannot match the style and fashionability of *la femme comme il faut*. As Susan Hiner explains, "The nearly invisible pronoun, the minuscule detail of grammar, like the fashion accessory in the grammar of clothing, makes all the difference, if one is capable of reading it" (10). Yet, as Hiner points out, Balzac's use of this pun indicates that while these two social types appear to be each other's foils, they are perhaps less distinct than one might think. For an in-depth analysis of Balzac's text and other nineteenth-century works about this type, see Hiner, especially chapter one.

[9] Béatrix, or Beatrice, appears as one of the guides in Dante Alighieri's *Divine Comedy* and was Dante's beloved.

out in all kinds of weather. She goes here and there. She trots about. She does not know whether she will or will not go into a shop. Whereas the proper woman knows exactly what she wants and what she is doing, the bourgeois woman is indecisive. She hikes up her dress to cross streams of sewage. She drags her child alongside her, which keeps her on the lookout for vehicles. She displays her motherhood in public, and she chats with her daughter. She has money in her purse and openwork stockings on her feet. In the winter, she wears a boa with her fur cape, and in summer, a shawl and a scarf. The bourgeois woman has mastered the art of redundant accessories.

You will see your Rambling Rose, if indeed you see her at all, at the Italiens, at the Opera, at a ball. There she appears so unique that you might say she is two different creations. The woman emerges from her mysterious outfit like a butterfly out of her silky cocoon. Like a delicacy to your delighted eyes, she shows off the forms that her bodice only barely suggested in the morning. At the theater, she never occupies seats above the second tier, except at the Italiens, so you can easily examine the studied slowness of her movements. The charming deceiver uses little strategic tricks known to all women with such a natural air so as to exclude any sense of artifice and premeditation.

If she happens to have a royally beautiful hand, even the shrewdest observer will believe that it is absolutely necessary for her to move back or move aside one of the ringlets or curls with which she is playing. If there is splendor in her profile, you will believe that she is saying something ironic or graceful to her neighbor while positioning herself in a way that produces a magnificent effect with her profile, so loved by great painters. Such a position attracts light upon the cheek, outlines the nose with a neat line, illuminates the pink of the nostrils, brings into sharp relief the ridges of her forehead, exposes the fiery specks of her eyes that gaze forward, and traces with light the round whiteness of her chin. If she has a lovely foot, she will throw herself on the sofa with the elegance of a kitten in the sunlight, her feet stretched out, and in such a way that you will not find anything in her attitude other than the most charming model ever lazily offered to a sculptor. Only the proper woman is fully comfortable even when she is all dolled up. Nothing bothers her. You will never catch her, as you might a bourgeois woman, fixing an uncooperative epaulette or pulling down the insubordinate whalebone of her corset or checking to see if the gorget[10] is fulfilling its duty as an unfaithful guardian of two glimmering white trea-

---

[10] An article of women's clothing covering the neck and breast.

sures, nor even catching a glimpse of herself in the mirror to make sure her hairstyle is staying in place. Her outfit is always in harmony with her character. She has had time to study it, to decide what suits her well, because she knows clearly what does not suit her. To be a proper woman, you don't need to be witty, but it's impossible to be one without having excellent taste. You will never see her exit the theater—she slips out before the end of the show. If by chance she appears upon the red steps of the staircase, she experiences violent emotions. She is there out of obligation. She has a few quick glances to cast, a few promises to receive. Perhaps she is coming down slowly so as to satisfy the vanity of a slave whom she occasionally obeys.

If you meet her at a ball or a party, you will perceive the sweetness of her sly voice, affected or natural. Her empty words will delight you, and she will know with a slight maneuver how to invest them with the value of deep thought. This woman's wit shows the success of strictly superficial art. You will not know what she said but you will be charmed by it. She nods her head or gently shrugs her white shoulders. She sprinkles her insignificant speech with a charming smile. She adds an epigram by Voltaire in an "eh!"—in an "ah!"—in an "oh, really!" A toss of her head is her most active form of questioning. Even the little movement with which she swings the perfume flask worn on her finger is significant.

She obtains great effect through the smallest of movements: a graceful hand gesture on the back of a chair, like dewdrops on a flower petal, and there is nothing left to say. She has rendered judgment without possibility of an appeal, even that which would move the most insensible of souls. She knows how to listen to you. She gives you the opportunity to be witty, and—here I appeal to your modesty—these moments are rare. You have not yet been shocked by a single questionable idea. You can't chat with a bourgeois woman for more than half an hour without her somehow mentioning her husband. With a proper woman, even if you know that she is married, she has the decency to conceal her husband's existence so well that you have to be a veritable Christopher Columbus to discover him. Sometimes you fail to discover him all by yourself. If you don't get a chance to ask anyone about this, by the end of the party you will surprise her in the act of looking fixedly at a middle-aged man with military decoration who bows and leaves. She asks for her carriage and departs. You are not the rose, but you were close to it, and you will sleep under the golden canopy of a delicious dream that will persist, perhaps even after Sleep uses its heavy finger to open up the ivory gates to the palace of fantasies.

At her house, no proper woman is available before four in the afternoon when she receives. She is clever enough to always make you wait. You will find everything in her house in excellent taste. The luxuries are fashionable and refreshed appropriately. You will see nothing behind glass, no rags hanging as in a pantry. You will feel warm going up the stairs. Everywhere flowers will attract your gaze—flowers are the only gift she accepts, and even then, only from certain people. The bouquets live just one day, bring pleasure, and must be replaced. For her, they are, as in the Orient, a symbol and a promise. Pricey, fashionable knickknacks are displayed, but not as in a museum or a curiosity shop. You will find her sitting on a loveseat by the fire, from which she will greet you without rising. Her conversation will not be the same as at the ball. Elsewhere, she was our creditor. At home, she owes you the pleasure of her wit. The proper woman has perfectly mastered these nuances. What she likes in you is a man who will expand her social circle, the object of great care and great concern for proper women today. Thus, in order to keep you in her salon, she will be ravishingly charming. This shows you how isolated women are nowadays, and why they want to have a small universe around them, at which they are the center. Conversation is impossible without generalities. The epigram—that novel contained in a single word—no longer strikes people or things, as it did in the eighteenth century, but it falls on petty events and lasts not even a day. Her wit, if she has it, consists in casting doubt on everything, just like the wit of a bourgeois woman is in affirming everything. Here lies the big difference between these two women: the bourgeois woman most certainly has virtue; the proper woman doesn't know whether she still has it or whether she will always have it. She hesitates and resists where the other flatly refuses and falls flat.

This hesitation about everything is one of the last charms that our terrible times have left her. She rarely goes to church, but she will talk of religion, and she will want to convert you if you have the good taste to be a free spirit, since you will have opened the door to the stereotypical phrases, to the haughty attitudes, and to the gestures agreed upon by these women. "Shame on you! I thought you had too much sense to attack religion! Society is crumbling, and you are taking away its support. As for religion, right now it's you and me, it's property, it's the future of our children. Ah! Let's not be selfish. Individualism is the sickness of our times, and religion is the only remedy for it. It brings together the families that your laws tear apart," and so on. She then launches into some neo-Christian speech, sprinkled with political ideas which are neither Catholic nor Protestant, but rather moral, oh so moral. In this speech, you will recognize a piece of every fabric woven by the modern doctrines that are all in conflict with one another. This speech shows that the proper woman represents an intellectual mess as well as a political one. Similarly, she is surrounded by glittering but not very solid products of an industry that constantly seeks to destroy its works in order to replace them with something new. You leave telling yourself, "Decidedly she has superior ideas!" You believe it all the more because she has probed your heart and your mind with her delicate hand, she has asked you your secrets, because the proper woman pretends to know nothing in order to learn everything. There are things that she never knows even when she knows them. But you are worried: you are unaware of the state of her heart.

In the olden days, noble women boasted their love affairs in newspapers and advertisements. These days, the proper woman has her little passions, orderly like a music sheet, with its eighth notes, its black and white keys, its quarter rests, its cadenza points, its sharp notes. A weak woman, she refuses to compromise her love, her husband, or her children's future. Today, a good name, a position, a fortune do not command enough respect to protect a woman's reputation. The aristocracy no longer comes forward en masse to shield a fallen woman.

Unlike the noble woman of the past, the proper woman does not engage in major battles. She cannot afford to crush anything with her little foot, lest it be she who is crushed. Thus, she is a woman of shrewd compromises, of the shiftiest temperament, of guarded decorum, steering her anonymous passions between two reef banks. She fears her servants as much as an Englishwoman fears being dragged to court for adultery. This woman, who is so free at the ball, so lovely on a walk, is a slave at home. She is independent only in private or in her own thoughts. She wants to remain a proper woman. This is her duty. For today, a woman abandoned by her husband, reduced to a meager allowance, with no carriage, no luxury, no opera boxes, no divine dress accessories, is no longer a woman or girl or even a bourgeois woman. She unravels and becomes a thing. The Carmelites[11] will not accept a married woman— that would be bigamy. Would her lover still want her? That is the question. The proper woman may give rise to slander, but never to a justified accusation. She lives between British hypocrisy and the gracious frankness of

---

[11] High-society ladies who retired to a convent often chose to join the Carmelite order.

the eighteenth century: an illegitimate system, typical
of an age when what comes next never resembles what
preceded it, where the transitions don't lead anywhere,
where grand figures fade away, and where distinctions
are purely personal.

I am convinced that it is impossible for a woman
before the age of twenty-five—even one born close to
the throne—to acquire the encyclopedic knowledge
of sweet nothings and tiny maneuvers, the grand little
things; the music of the voice and the harmony of colors; the angelic mischief and the innocent cunning; the
chatter and the silence; the seriousness and the banter;
the wit and the silliness; the diplomacy and the igno-
rance, which make up the proper woman. Some tactless
individuals have asked us if a female author is a proper
woman: when she is without talent, she is improper
indeed.[12]

So, who is this woman? To what family does she belong? From where does she hail? This is where the proper
woman takes on truly revolutionary proportions. She is
a modern creation, a deplorable triumph of the elective
system applied to the fair sex. Every revolution has its

---

[12] In the French version, Balzac uses the expression "c'est une femme
comme il n'en faut pas." Playing on a proper woman's transformation
into an improper one by the simple addition of "en," Balzac conveys
here the idea that a woman writer without talent is not useful.

own word, a word that sums it up and represents it. To explain certain words, added century after century to the French language, would be to write a magnificent history. For example, the word "to organize" describes the Empire—it contains Napoleon in his entirety. For the last fifty years, we have witnessed a continuous destruction of all social distinctions. We should have saved our women from this monumental shipwreck, but the Civil Code[13] has unleashed its leveling articles upon their heads. Alas! As awful as these words are, we must say them: the duchesses are vanishing and so are the marquises. As for the baronesses, they have never been taken seriously. Aristocracy begins with the viscountesses. The countesses are here to stay. Every proper woman is, more or less, a countess: a countess of the Empire or of yesteryear, a countess of old stock or, as they say in Italian, a countess by courtesy.

As for the noble woman, she has vanished, along with all the accoutrements of the last century: the powder, the beauty spots, the high heels, the wire corsets

---

[13] The Civil Code (or Napoleonic Code) was established under Napoleon I in 1804. It unified previously disparate feudal laws into one system. Balzac refers to the erasure of social distinctions in the aftermath of the French Revolution, an erasure that continued under Napoleon. According to Balzac, this break with traditional hierarchies has occasioned the emergence of new social codes.

bedecked with ribbons. Today's duchesses can pass through doors without needing to widen them because of their pannier skirts.[14] The Empire witnessed the end of dresses with trains! I have a hard time figuring out why a sovereign who wished to have his court swept by silk and velour dresses with trains didn't establish indestructible laws of birthright. Napoleon could never have imagined the repercussions of the Code of which he was so proud. By creating his duchesses, this man engendered the proper women, a byproduct of his legislation. Both school-aged children and obscure journalists alike deployed this new concept to demolish the magnificence of social status. Today, every rogue who can suitably hold his head straight in his collar, cover his manly chest with a yard of satin for body armor, display a forehead where apocryphal genius flickers under his curls, prance about in patent-leather high heels with silk stockings that cost six francs, hold his eyeglass over his eye by wrinkling his cheek—be he a mere notary's clerk

---

[14] The pannier skirts, or skirts with large hoops, fashionable in the eighteenth century, were so large that their wearers occasionally had trouble getting through doorways. In his 1721 epistolary novel *Lettres persanes* (*Persian Letters*), Montesquieu playfully suggests that architects had to modify doors' structure to accommodate pannier skirts. Unlike nineteenth-century crinoline wearers, however, ladies wearing pannier skirts would never be seen walking on the street.

or a businessman's son or a banker's bastard, he can impertinently look up and down the prettiest of duchesses, size her up as she walks down the stairs at the theater, and say to his friend whose trousers come from Blain, whose coat comes from Buisson, and whose vest, glove, and ties come from Bodier or Perry,[15] "That, my dear, is a proper woman."

As for the reasons for this disaster, here they are. Any duke of the sort one could find under Louis XVIII or Charles X[16] who had an income of two hundred thousand livres a year, a magnificent mansion, and a sumptuous domestic staff could still live like a great lord. The last one of these great lords in France, the Prince of Talleyrand, has just died.[17] He left four children, including two daughters. Assuming that every one of his heirs married well, each of them now only has an income of one hundred thousand livres a year. Each of them is a parent to several children and is obliged to live on a tight budget in a first- or second-floor apartment.[18] Who

---

[15] Names of fashionable Parisian clothing and accessory makers.

[16] Louis XVIII and Charles X, the two brothers of the guillotined king Louis XVI, were the last two kings of the Bourbon monarchy.

[17] Charles-Maurice de Talleyrand was a French statesman who held high office under several successive regimes (French Revolution, Napoleon I, Restoration). He was known for his political shrewdness.

[18] In this passage, Balzac alludes to changes in family and inheritance laws enacted since the French Revolution. Primogeniture of inheritance (a custom whereby the oldest son inherits the entire estate) was

even knows whether they are hunting a fortune? From then on, the eldest son's wife is a duchess in name only: she has no carriage, no servants, no theater box, no free time. She has no rooms of her own in the mansion, no fortune, and no trinkets. She is buried in her marriage the way a woman from the Rue Saint-Denis is buried in her commerce. She buys stockings for her dear little children, nurses them herself, and watches over her daughters, whom she no longer sends to be educated in a convent. And just like that, the noblest woman becomes a respectable homemaker.

In our times, those beautiful, feminine flowers that decorated the great centuries of the past no longer exist. The noble woman's fan is broken. Today's woman no longer needs to blush, to gossip, to whisper, to hide or reveal herself. Now the fan is used only to fan oneself, and when an object becomes only that which it actually is, it is too useful to be an object of luxury. Everything in France has colluded against the proper woman.

The aristocrats have accepted this situation by seeking refuge in their estates, where they are hiding in order to die, retreating before new ideas just as they retreated

---

first abolished in 1791. The Napoleonic Code of 1804 codified this into law that entitled all children born in a marriage to an equal share of inheritance. Some proponents of the old custom, such as Balzac, saw it as destabilizing the economic unity of families.

abroad from the revolutionary masses. The women who could have founded European salons, who could have formed opinions and then changed them as if they were gloves, who could have ruled the world by ruling men of arts or ideas—these women made an error by ceding the terrain. Too ashamed were they to fight with the bourgeoisie intoxicated by power and to emerge onto the world scene just to be chopped up into pieces by those barbarians who followed closely at their heels. So, where the bourgeois wishes to see princesses, we can see only proper young women. Today's princes can't find any more noble women to compromise; they can't even bestow distinction upon a woman taken off the street. The Duke of Bourbon was the last prince to use this privilege, and God knows what that cost him![19] These days, princes are married to proper women who are obliged to share an opera box with their friends and who will not gain anything from royal favor. They float unnoticeably between the waters of the bourgeois class and that of the nobility: they are not entirely noble, but not

---

[19] Louis Henri Joseph de Bourbon, prince de Condé, took as his mistress a woman who had been a maid in a bordello. He attempted to give her respectability by marrying her off to an aristocrat. Balzac's text refers to the fact that Louis Henri died under suspicious circumstances, presumably murdered.

quite bourgeois. The press has supplanted such women. They no longer have the benefit of the art of conversation: those delicious calumnies, bedecked in beautiful language. Instead, there are articles written in a dialect that changes every three years, and little newspapers that are as amusing as a mortician and as light as their leaden font.[20] What were once French conversations are now conducted in a revolutionary patois from one end of

---

[20] Here Balzac expresses his disdain for the quality of the contemporary press.

France to another, printed in long columns in mansions where the printing press has replaced the brilliant salons of yesteryear. Do you hear the death knell of high society? Its first stroke is the proper woman of today! This woman, hailing from the ranks of the nobility or emerging from the bourgeoisie, a product of every soil, even the provinces, is the expression of modern times, the last incarnation of good taste, of wit, of grace, of distinction, all combined but diminished. We will no longer see a noble woman in France, but we will have proper women for a long time, elected by public opinion to the upper chamber of women, and who will be for the fair sex what the gentleman is in England. This is what we call progress: in the past, a woman might have had the voice of a herring-monger, a grenadier's gait, the face of a courtesan, a receding hairline, big feet, thick hands—and yet she could still be a noble woman. But today, even if she were a Montmorency[21] (if ever a Montmorency could be this way), she would not be a proper woman.

---

[21] Montmorency was one of the oldest and most distinguished names in France.

Louis Huart

Physiology of the Grisette

Louis Huart was a prolific author of physiologies *who also wrote journalistic works for the satirical newspaper* Le charivari. *He produced numerous plays and eventually became the director of the Théâtre National de l'Odéon and the founder of the Théâtre des Folies-Nouvelles. Most* physiologies *contain between thirteen and sixteen chapters. For this volume, we have selected those that illustrate particularly clearly the salient characteristics of the type in question and help construct a full picture of the character.*

Chapter 2: In Which the Author Tackles His Subject in Earnest

Our modern grisettes are not the first ones to have been appreciated, courted, and "physiologized."[1] Two hundred years ago, one of our greatest poets dedicated the following verses to them, verses that, despite having been written during Louis XIV's era, are not especially rococo:

> A grisette is a treasure
> And without any effort at all
> And without taking her to the ball
> You easily make her your pleasure.

---

[1] Huart creates a neologism here. For more on the phenomenon of the *physiologies*, see the Introduction.

> Your effort does not have to be plentiful,
> The hard thing is finding one who is faithful.[2]

Today's grisette bears a certain resemblance to the one our dear La Fontaine wrote about. She is still a treasure, if you will, but you really have to put in the effort. Otherwise, no chance. You will never get what you want. Tell her whatever you want—she always believes it. As for fidelity—she has just as much of it as certain high-society women, with all due respect.

The same is true for the grisette as it is for a whole host of excellent things that come and go. If things continue along these lines, there will be nothing good left. The grisette—the real one, not the fake one—is a young girl between the ages of sixteen and thirty who sews or embroiders all week and who plays on Sundays. From the time she is thirty until the most remote old age, she loses her specialty. She may be a dressmaker, a maker of undergarments, a florist, a milliner, a burnisher, an embroiderer, or a chambermaid. But after this point, there will be nothing special about her.

---

[2] This citation is a slightly modified excerpt from Jean de La Fontaine's work *Joconde*, in which he writes, "Une grisette est un trésor; / Car, sans se donner de la peine, / Et sans qu'aux bals on la promène, / On en vient aisément à bout; / On lui dit ce qu'on veut, bien souvent rien du tout, / Le point est d'en trouver une qui soit fidèle" (301).

Good, kindhearted, funny, and devoted, the grisette is a unique mixture of the most opposite of qualities. She certainly has her faults. Man was not born perfect, as a policeman once said. The grisette was also not born perfect, but with her, the good qualities outweigh all the others.

Woman's fate on earth is not always the happiest. Although some gentleman whose name we can no longer remember once said that Paris was hell for horses and paradise for women, it is hardly certain that the grisette has ever experienced the joys of paradise found in the capital city.[3] She sometimes has her joyful moments, but oh so many sad quarter hours, so to speak!

On her own from a young age, the poor child, upon leaving her apprenticeship, gets set up in her *à part* (her apartment, in the French of the grisette, the painter's apprentice, and the student): a trundle bed, a mattress, a chair, a glass, and a water pitcher make up her furnishings. She is lucky if the room is even big enough for all these objects. She overlooks the roofs of the surrounding building, and you can easily recognize the window of

---

[3] This is a reference to the French proverb "Paris est l'enfer des chevaux, le purgatoire des hommes, et le paradis des femmes" 'Paris is hell for horses, purgatory for men, and paradise for women.'

her modest apartment by the copious nasturtiums that frame it.

The high-society lady has great contempt for the grisette. She cannot forgive her lovely foot, her dainty and elegant waist, and her sweet little face. What makes her even more furious is that the grisette is completely unaware of the jealousy she inspires.

Carefree and disinterested, the grisette never thinks about the future. She imagines that life will always be as it is at that very moment. She imagines that her Adolphe[4] will always be with her and will never abandon her. Little does she know that in a few short months, her sweetheart will leave her for a woman of higher rank, even if this new mistress is not worth her little finger. This fickle woman will more than avenge the grisette, so cruelly and harshly abandoned by her lover—but let's not get ahead of ourselves!

Chapter 5: The Grisette's Passions

Nothing is perfect on this earth, and if you look really closely, you will find that spring is not always full of roses, that Odry's nose[5] is a little too large, and that a

---

[4] Adolphe is a stereotypical name for an unfaithful young lover, taken from the hero of the 1816 novel *Adolphe* by Benjamin Constant.
[5] Jacques Charles Odry was a comedic actor, playwright, and poet who often performed in popular theatrical works and was known

simple broth that a poor person might consume is not nourishing enough unless you add a large roast and potatoes to it. So why would you assume that the grisette would be without some minor shortcomings?

She too has her passions, but they are fairly innocent and for the most part easy to satisfy.

When a phrenologist[6] examines a grisette (only her head, naturally), the first lump that he encounters is the one that represents chestnuts, rum babas, pancakes, mulled wine, and other similar treats.

Those who claim to be well informed insist that it was love that brought down Troy. This is quite possible, but it is most certainly chestnuts that spell doom for many Parisian grisettes.

Among people of high society, a suitor wouldn't dream of courting a lady without first offering her a bouquet of rare flowers. Among grisettes, the best way for a

---

for the size and prominence of his nose. Odry was also a name used frequently in French puns in the nineteenth century, for example: "Voyant un homme qui avait le nez très-gros, Odry disait: — En faisant cet homme-là la nature a fait un nez fort" 'After seeing a man with a big nose, Odry said, "When she made that man, Nature made a real effort"'—a play on words because "un nez fort" sounds like "an effort" in French. See Bara.

[6] Phrenology is a pseudoscientific discipline focused on measurements of the human skull that was popular in the early nineteenth century. According to phrenology, certain brain areas have specific functions.

young man to start things off is with fruit. The grisette
will savor three oranges and a bag of chestnuts infinitely
more than the most magnificent camellias.

Note that the difference in price is entirely in favor
of the grisette's suitor: eighteen cents instead of twenty
francs is substantial—even for a law student.

The suitor who announces his arrival to a shop or a
gathering of grisettes by a general distribution of oranges
and chestnuts is immediately declared *a proper young
man*, and the grisette who is the recipient of such tributes
tells herself that she will most certainly be happy with
such a charming gentleman.

From a very young age, the grisette has conducted
such an in-depth study of chestnuts that she immediately
recognizes the city or rather the countryside that produced it. She cannot be fooled by a seller, even the wiliest
one, trying to pass off a simple chestnut as a top-quality
Lyon chestnut.[7]

If, sometime in the winter, you get a sudden case of
the munchies, all you need to do is search a grisette's
pocket. Since her pocket serves as both her pantry and
her sewing bag, you would be mighty unlucky not to
unearth a dozen smoldering chestnuts, accompanied by

---

[7] A chestnut, not necessarily from Lyon, but called "de Lyon" because chestnuts were often shipped from Lyon after being harvested
from nearby regions.

half a brioche with currants and raisins, a piece of candy cane, a small sewing case, a few hazelnuts, three pralines, a thimble, and a crawfish leg.

During the summer, the grisette—deprived of chestnuts—indulges in rum babas when she is offered one or galettes when she has no gallant suitor.

From the Boulevard Montmartre to the Boulevard du Temple, there are at least eight or ten famous galette sellers. When the grisette walks the entire way, she feels compelled to make a little stop at each one of these establishments—especially if she is walking with a friend. This way they take turns treating themselves to a galette for two pennies apiece so that each one only puts in five centimes. While savoring this firm pastry, they engage in high-level gastronomical discussions on the comparative merits of the Gymnase galettes[8] and those from Porte-Saint-Denis.[9] It's a veritable comparative lecture on the galette.

While the Gymnase galette has many ardent admirers, the galettes from Porte-Saint-Denis also have fanatic supporters. But on this point the majority of grisettes adhere

---

[8] The Galette du Gymnase, located near the Théâtre du Gymnase in what is now the tenth arrondissement, was at that time one of the most famous places to purchase galettes.

[9] Another galette stand; also located in the tenth arrondissement, it would have been close to the Galette du Gymnase.

to the philosophy of eclecticism: that is, they consume with equal appetite the products of both famous rivals.

Moreover, to prove that Parisian grisettes devour enormous numbers of galettes, suffice it to say that the galette sellers make a real fortune in four or five years. Their merchandise sells out at exorbitant prices.

Take, for example, the merchant from Porte-Saint-Denis, who sells 150 meters of galette daily! That's 22,000 meters a year!

Of these, at least 20,000 meters are digested by grisettes, who hide a cast-iron stomach under their corsets. Firemen don't eat the galettes—they can't digest them.

Another passion, but this time a much less unhealthy one, and one shared by all grisettes, is a passion for the gillyflower![10]

There is likely not a single florist, milliner, seamstress, or laundress who has not devoted herself to horticulture by re-creating the hanging gardens of Babylon[11] on the window of her attic room in a three-by-eight-inch planter.

And the flower chosen by the grisette to embellish her life and her windowsill is inevitably the gillyflower.

---

[10] A genre of flowering plant known for its pleasant odor. Some examples include carnations, wallflowers, and stock.
[11] The Hanging Gardens of Babylon, tiered gardens that were known as one of the seven wonders of the ancient world.

The aforementioned gillyflower is watered morning and night with a full watering can. But, as we know from Monsieur de Buffon,[12] since the gillyflower is not able to absorb two pints of water a day, the result is that

---

[12] Georges-Louis Leclerc, comte de Buffon, was a famous French naturalist and the author of *Histoire naturelle* (1749; *Natural History*). He also served as the director of the Jardin des Plantes.

three-quarters of this water intended for the flower ends up watering the head of the neighbor on the floor below.

This daily watering leads to numerous recriminations from this neighbor, despite the fact that the turf on his head could only benefit from such an aquatic regimen (again, according to Monsieur de Buffon).

And finally, the third passion common among grisettes consists in their strong affection for brown and blonde mustaches . . . But let's stop right here! . . . This could lead us much too far—because this is no longer about agriculture!

Chapter 7: The Grisette's Literary and Political Opinions

The grisette, whose only true happiness is her freedom, unfailingly applies this extreme independence to her style and her spelling.

Thanks to the enlightenment that graced all social classes, every grisette knows how to write at least halfway legibly. But this playful young girl usually throws off the oppressive yoke of standard spelling rules and enjoys bringing together an off-the-cuff collection of letters that would prove deeply satisfying to Monsieur Marle,[13] the

---

[13] The author of the 1826 *Journal grammatical et didactique de la langue française, rédigé par M. Marle, membre de l'Athénée, de la Société grammaticale, etc., etc., et par plusieurs autres grammariens* (Grammatical and

langwich reeformer, and Monsieur Trubert,[14] the director of the Vaudeville, who gives out *orkestrah seets.*

Neither the grisette's head nor her fingers get even the most familiar words straight. Instead of *rendez-vous* she inevitably writes *randaivou,* unless she is also very pretentious, in which case she divides the word into three parts: *rang-dez-vou. Performance* inevitably becomes *parformanse* and *love* always has an extra *u* in the middle.

Maybe it's because the grisette always sharpens her quill with her scissors.

There is one word that would cause the grisette's despair if she ever bothered to despair about anything—and that's the word *polytechnique!*

Every time a grisette, even if she is a fancy milliner from the Rue Vivienne, finds herself in a friendly or commercial relationship with a student from the École Polytechnique,[15] she gets a severe migraine trying to

---

Didactic Journal of the French Language, edited by Mr. Marle, Member of the Athénée Society, of the Grammatical Society, etc. etc., and by Several Other Grammarians) and the 1829 *Réforme de l'orthographe actuelle de la langue française (Reform of Contemporary Spelling of the French Language),* Marle proposed a radical reformation of French spelling in which words would be written as they were pronounced.

[14] Trubert was the director of the popular Théâtre du Vaudeville during the July Monarchy. He was rumored to have grossly misspelled *orchestre* as "orquestre" and *places* as "plasses." See Simond.

[15] The École Polytechnique, located in what is now the fifth arrondissement, in the Latin Quarter, where it was relocated by Napoleon in 1804.

write the address on a love letter destined to the student at said school. No matter how hard she tries, there is no way her assemblage of *S*'s, *H*'s, and *Y*'s will align to produce the desired *polytechnique*. This makes the hardest brainteaser look like child's play.

And thus many grisettes owe the reputation of modesty and virtue that they enjoy at the École Polytechnique to the involuntary silence they are obliged to keep vis-à-vis their boyfriends who declare their love via the post and who beg them to respond in kind.

Thankfully, remnants of that old and very useful guild of public scribes are still in existence, those saviors of kitchen cooks who like to keep two copies of their records, and of young seamstresses whom heaven has endowed with a sensitive heart, and who consequently cannot bear to see a handsome young man suffer, whether he has blond or dark hair (or even two young men, one blond and another dark). Therefore, just like the kitchen cook, the grisette also keeps two copies of her correspondence.

At least the public scribe doesn't make too many careless mistakes in his spelling. His style is always commensurate with the circumstances. And he is even willing, when needed, to respond in verse, for just five pennies more.

Then he signs the whole thing "Virginie" or "José-phine" in beautiful cursive letters, with lots of pomp, circumstance, and gold powder—unless it's tobacco instead. Employing a public scribe has a double advantage. On the one hand, it boosts one's self-esteem. On the other, it provides a cover in case the correspondence is confiscated: you can always deny that the writing and the tobacco are yours and claim your innocence by pretending to pull your hair out. Because it is an accepted fact that hair pulling is proof of one's innocence.

That's all for the grisette's writing. As for her reading, thanks to an in-depth study of the best authors that she has conducted since her early childhood, she is well read, especially of course when it comes to books in print.

Thus the grisette is usually pretty up-to-date on all the contemporary authors. When she is asked whether she prefers Victor Hugo or Balzac, she quickly responds: "Paul de Kock!"[16]

---

[16] Paul de Kock (see Introduction) was a prolific author of novels, short stories, *physiologies*, and vaudevilles. His name became a symbol of popular literature of dubious quality ("industrial literature," a term coined in 1839 by the critic Charles Augustin Sainte-Beuve in the essay "De la littérature industrielle") and was often reviewed negatively by literary critics. Though de Kock found many readers among the petite bourgeoisie and the upper classes, he was often referred to as the author most favored by grisettes, and the figure of the grisette is featured prominently throughout his oeuvre.

According to the grisette, the author of *My Neighbor Raymond*[17] is the greatest novelist of modern times. He eclipses Eugène Sue, George Sand, Frédéric Soulié, and even Balzac,[18] because the grisette is only capable of appreciating literature that's amusing, and nothing amuses her more than love stories and bawdy jokes. Virtuous novels like the ones by Ducray-Duminil[19] don't appeal to her at all. She points out that in these works, virtue is much too unrealistic.

----

[17] Published in 1842, *Mon voisin Raymond* is one of Paul de Kock's best-known novels.

[18] Eugène Sue was best known for his serial novel *Les mystères de Paris* (1842–1843; *The Mysteries of Paris*). At the time of the *Physiologie de la grisette*'s publication, Sue had not yet published *Mysteries*, but his novel of manners, *Mathilde* (1840–1841), was being serialized in the newspaper *La presse* (*The Press*) and was extremely popular. George Sand (Amandine Aurore Lucile Dupin) was a prolific writer of novels, short stories, plays, and autobiographical works, including *Indiana* (1832), *Consuelo* (1843), and *La petite Fadette* (1849; *Little Fadette*). Frédéric Soulié was a popular novelist, journalist, and playwright during the July Monarchy. He also contributed to the *physiologie* phenomenon with his 1841 *Physiologie du bas-bleu* (*Physiology of the Bluestocking*). Honoré de Balzac was a writer best known for his masterpiece *La comédie humaine* (*The Human Comedy*). When Huart's *physiologie* was published in 1841, Balzac was already the celebrated author of many novels, including *La peau de chagrin* (1831; *The Magic Skin*), *Le père Goriot* (1835; *Old Goriot*), and *Le colonel Chabert* (1835). His 1829 publication *La physiologie du mariage* (*Physiology of Marriage*) was thought by some to be the inspiration for the later *physiologie* series.

[19] François Guillaume Ducray-Duminil was a French writer for children and young adults in the late eighteenth and early nineteenth centuries. He was especially known for the virtuousness and innocence promoted in his works.

She'll tell you this with the greatest composure, while lacing up her boots.

And so the publication of a new work by Paul de Kock always has the biggest impact in Parisian stores. The best thing a chivalrous young man can do is to immediately procure the latest novel by Paul de Kock for the grisette he is trying to woo. This will make for a very enjoyable evening . . . with the novel, that is.

The grisette neglects the fine arts much more than literature. She only vaguely knows the names of Paul Delaroche, Pradier, or David.[20] But she gladly stops to admire the statuettes by Dantan;[21] this even gives her the opportunity to turn around quickly toward another admirer of this witty caricaturist and call him "naughty."

I have no idea what he might have said or done to her, but it is a fact that she responds, "You naughty thing!"

---

[20] Hippolyte de la Roche, or Paul Delaroche, was a French painter famous for his *juste milieu* paintings, a style from the July Monarchy seen as reconciling classicism and romanticism. James or Jean-Jacques Pradier was a Swiss-born sculptor and painter who worked in France. Jacques-Louis David was a French neoclassical painter, known for his paintings before the French Revolution, his works documenting the Revolution, and his portraits of Napoleon.

[21] Jean-Pierre Dantan (Dantan le Jeune) was a French sculptor known for his caricatural renderings of contemporary politicians, artists, and writers. He is said to have inspired the renowned artist and caricaturist Honoré Daumier.

What on earth could have happened to her? But enough of that, we've dwelled on the subject for far too long, and after all it's none of our business.

The grisette who has relationships with artists is easy to spot. She sprinkles her speech with art studio terms, especially around the times of art exhibitions, and she is infinitely flattered when she sees her portrait hanging in a big gallery next to that of a captain in full regalia. To this last point, many high-society ladies are just like grisettes. Thankfully, nowadays the grisette can obtain the satisfaction of a *daguerreotype* portrait.[22]

But what would flatter the grisette so much more would be to have her statuette made! Consequently, there are few sculptors out there who are not bombarded by such requests. They usually get rid of their solicitors by assuring them that the statuettes, when first made, are dressed like the statues in the Tuilerie gardens, and that it is not until the eighteenth modeling session that they acquire clothing.

The solicitor blushes and drops her request, because even milliners can be virtuous.

----

[22] This technique, in which a picture is recorded on a silvered copper plate, was introduced by Louis-Jacques-Mandé Daguerre in 1839 and remained the most successful commercial photographic process until 1860.

In general, the grisette doesn't care much for politics. When you spend your week making two hats, sewing three dresses, creasing five bonnets, and making 885,736 mattress stitches, you simply don't have the leisure to worry about Méhémet-Ali[23] or the queen of Spain or another monarch who has the right and the pleasure of placing his plaster bust on the mantel of all of the kingdom's civil servants.

So the grisette must associate with an ardent republican to have even the slightest notion of human rights. Of all possible political activities, there is only one that she likes well enough—I am talking about the one where you toast to various freedoms with cider and mulled wine! Especially when mulled wine is involved, over the course of the same evening she would drink to the health of Louis-Philippe, the duke of Bordeaux, the republic, the sultan, and the pasha of Egypt!

Chapter 15: The Grisette's Ultimate Reincarnation

Monsieur de Balzac claims, or at least used to claim a few years ago, that thirty is the best age for women.[24]

---

[23] Muhammad Ali, ruler of Egypt from 1805 to 1848.
[24] A reference to Balzac's novel *La femme de trente ans* (*A Woman of Thirty*), written between 1829 and 1842.

This principle may be correct in general, but it most certainly does not apply to the grisette. Because at twenty-nine she is a sorry sight, and at thirty, the grisette no longer exists.

These lugubrious words do not mean that, having arrived at this critical age, the grisette necessitates the services of a funeral home. Not at all, far from it, because in fact she has never been as plump and round as she is at that age. But she is no longer plump and round like a grisette, but rather like a vest-maker, a linen seller, a haberdasher, and these are not at all the same thing. As we have already noted at the beginning of this volume, the young girl has vanished and has transformed herself into a more or less fresh young woman, with more or less whitish teeth, but who is most certainly not the cheerful grisette with whom you danced a few years ago. Transformation, transmutation, and reincarnation have occurred. She is orderly and economical. Sometimes she has a husband, and almost always she has children to whom, whether or not she is married, she teaches lessons in virtue as though she had done this sort of thing all her life.

What's more, out of twenty grisettes there are at most five who reach the age of thirty without losing the necessary grisette qualifications. Because between the ages of twenty and twenty-five, three become Lorettes,[25] four or five buy a shop using various savings, and seven or eight become tinsmiths, wholesale wine merchants, or grocers, with a husband blessed by Monsieur the mayor!

Because even if, at twenty-five, the grisette enjoys it when someone whispers sweet nothings in her ear, she becomes prim and proper to those who let on that they would go out with her if she made it worth their while.

In this case, she deploys the kind of diplomatic savvy that would do honor to a disciple of Monsieur de Talleyrand[26] and dispenses a gigantic smack to the brave soul who had the temerity merely to squeeze the tips of her fingers.

And the suitor, who is completely oblivious, immediately and legitimately offers her his heart, his hand, and his bottles. She accepts all of it.

Once married, the grisette is usually a good wife, a good mother, and a good wine (or whatever) merchant.

---

[25] Named after the Parisian neighborhood Notre-Dame-de-Lorette, where many of them lived, the Lorettes were young women who straddled the line between the grisette and the kept woman. Like the grisette, the Lorette figured frequently in popular culture and earned her own *Physiologie de la Lorette* (1841), by Maurice Alhoy.

[26] Charles-Maurice de Talleyrand was a French statesman who held high office under several successive regimes (French Revolution, Napoleon I, Restoration). He was known for his political shrewdness.

She is much less susceptible to the flirtations of the admirers who loiter around her counter because her youth was so tempestuous. Nothing like personal experience to get to know what men are really all about!

As for the grisette who, thanks to her astute maneuvers, manages to marry a nice little bourgeois who has a nice little thousand livres of income—which is not rare—she promptly loses her happy and original grisette nature and takes on instead the much less happy nature of a bourgeoise.

This means that she is awfully nitpicky with her cook and acts like a princess with her *marchande de mode*.[27] It goes without saying that she only calls them "honey," or even "hon."

She gives all her affection to her husband, whom she calls "my big pet," which does not prevent her from threatening to gouge his eyes out every time he dares smile at the servant girl, even if it's just to ask her for some shaving water. At thirty-five, the grisette-turned-bourgeoise has so well satisfied her love of good food that she becomes deplorably obese. At forty, a portrait of

---

[27] *Marchande de mode* was a term that referred to high-end seamstresses, hat and headpiece makers, dress embellishers, purveyors of fashionable items, and what can be described today as "stylists." These *marchandes de mode* competed with regular seamstresses for elite clientele. They had more freedom than seamstresses, who were constrained by the tailor's guild.

her engraved in wood could serve as an advertisement for the precious Arab *racahout*.[28]

As for the grisette who becomes neither a bourgeoise nor a married woman nor a shopkeeper nor a Lorette— that grisette inevitably becomes an excessively pious and no less mean old maid. At the age of fifty, she almost always affiliates herself with the Congregation of the Blessed Virgin Mary.[29]

But why even bother worrying about what will become of the old grisette? Do we worry, in May, about what will become of the lovely rosebuds that greet our eyes and fill the air with their fragrance? Every year, a crop of fresh and cheerful grisettes comes to replace the old one. In France, the grisettes are like royalty—they can never be extinguished.

At the end of the last carnival season, you noticed with chagrin that a few of the usual dancers at the ball were starting to get crow's feet. Go to this year's opening dances and you will find two hundred lively, fresh things

---

[28] This nutritional powder made of starches, sugar, and cacao was highly advertised in the early nineteenth century and appeared in other *physiologies* and vaudevilles. Presumably the grisette, by the age of forty, has grown so corpulent that she could serve as an appropriate advertisement for this nourishing supplement.

[29] The former grisette's membership in this charitable lay order would attest to her prudishness in middle age.

that have just escaped from the shops of Herbaut,[30] Palmyre,[31] Victorine, etc., etc.

And, just like the royal courtiers in charge of hailing the advent of a new king, you will exclaim:

The grisette is dead, long live the grisette!

---

[30] A fashionable hat shop situated on the Rue Neuve-Saint-Augustin.

[31] Madame Palmyre was a famous dressmaker. The Empress Eugénie, a fashion trendsetter and the wife of Napoleon III, later became one of her clients.

LOUIS HUART

Physiology of the Flâneur

In early-nineteenth-century literature, the word flâneur *first appeared without the circumflex. Initially, this urban personage had almost universally negative connotations of a lazy idler. The change in spelling accompanied a change in connotation and valence. As Priscilla Parkhurst Ferguson writes, "The term soon climbs the lexicographical and social ladder. The circumflex accent that the word usually acquires signals a redefinition through a change of perspective. Instead of prompting a negative moral judgement, the flâneur's conspicuous inaction comes to be taken as positive evidence of both social status and superior thought" (Paris as Revolution 82–83). This work, originally published as* Physiologie du flaneur, *must have appeared on the cusp of this transition.*

Chapter 2: Can Anyone Be a Flâneur?

"Nothing more common than the name, but nothing more rare than the thing," said La Fontaine about true friends.[1] The same can be said about true flâneurs. And if from the definition of man we gave in the previous chapter you concluded that all men were destined to become flâneurs, you would be sorely mistaken.

There are the unfortunate individuals who, for one reason or another, are deprived of the ability to taste the

---

[1] Jean de La Fontaine was French writer particularly well known for his fables.

pleasures of flânerie, a pleasure that we do not hesitate to call that of the gods, for the gods of Olympus often disguised themselves so that they could practice flânerie at will on earth, like good little rentiers,[2] after having partaken of their half-cup of ambrosia, the coffee of the time.[3]

To begin with, there are various invalids who cannot possibly engage in flânerie. There is little charm in walking on the Terrasse des Feuillants[4] when you're a patient at the Quinze-Vingts,[5] or in wandering in the Tuileries when you suffer from a huge protrusion in the middle of your back—you run the risk of being stopped at the gates by an infantry soldier who strictly abides by his orders not to let any large packages into the park.

Those who walk with a limp can only venture out by carriage. Those who have the misfortune of being deaf risk being run over by vehicles while walking on the boulevards. As you can see, to bear the title of *flâneur*, a rare combination of physical qualities is absolutely

---

[2] A rentier was a man who lived off the revenues of his business or property but who himself did not have to work. He was often an object of derision in the literature of the time.

[3] Huart maps references to Greek mythology (here, ambrosia, the drink of the Greek gods) onto the emerging café culture.

[4] A fashionable place to walk in the Jardin des Tuileries.

[5] A hospital for the blind.

indispensable. It's even more than what's required for the military's draft board.

And let's not forget about the many requisite moral qualities, to which we shall return later on.

We almost overlooked a class of unfortunate people for whom flânerie is only possible during those temperate months when oysters are safe to eat[6]—that is, the excessively portly and naturally stout flâneurs. As soon as the first rays of sunlight of May pierce the clouds, the obese flâneur finds himself the unluckiest of men! He tries, in vain, to struggle against his destiny. No sooner has he taken three or four hundred steps on the boulevard's sidewalk than he loses all his determination. All he can do is stumble onto a chair in the nearest café and mop his brow. And to cool down, this imprudent man guzzles two or three bottles of beer—his most treacherous and fattening enemy.

People afflicted with fifty thousand livres of private income can never know the bliss that a simple walk in the mud of Paris can bring. These Turcarets[7] would consider themselves forever compromised if they got even a

---

[6] Customarily, oysters are not consumed during hot summer months for fear of food poisoning.

[7] The eponymous character of Alain-René Lesage's 1709 play *Turcaret, ou le financier* (*Turcaret; or, The Financier*) is a vulgar state financial adviser who only cares about money.

bit splattered. But they are truly punished for their vanity by the ennui they experience in splattering others.

The lanterns on the Place de la Concorde, the Arc de Triomphe, and the stunted and dusty trees of the Bois de Boulogne[8] surely appear monotonous when they are contemplated 365 times a year from the back of a carriage or even from the heights of a more or less Arabian horse. Yet this is the only point of view offered by a walk in the Bois de Boulogne. If this type of entertainment is all you get, it's almost better not to have money. But we would not recommend pushing this worldview to the point of incurring any debts, because this would be going to the opposite extreme and would bring up a whole host of other problems.

The flâneur who has creditors finds himself denied the enjoyment of numerous streets, riverbanks, squares, and shopping arcades. He must carefully study the topography of Paris. He should assiduously avoid the Rue de Richelieu,[9] for there he risks meeting his tailor, who, having grown tired of waiting to receive at least some payment for his services, could completely block his way with a large bill.

---

[8] Parisian spots frequented by elegant society.
[9] The Rue de Richelieu, in the first arrondissement, was one of the most fashionable streets of Paris during the first half of the nineteenth century.

Nor is the Rue Saint-Honoré safe,[10] for there dwells a ferocious boot maker who swore to drink your blood until it totaled the 557 francs you owe him. Avoid the Rue Saint-Honoré if you do not wish to provide this parched cannibal a lemonade from your veins.

Further along is the hatmaker's street, then the glovemaker's, etc., etc. In other words, in order to get from the Palais-Royal to the Place de la Bourse, our unfortunate man is sometimes required to take a huge detour via the Rue Grenetat and the Place Royale, so sprinkled with dangerous barricades are these other streets.[11]

If the reckless debtor has signed a promissory note to a moneylender, his position becomes entirely untenable and he must give up flânerie altogether, as long as the sun has not set and the lampposts are not lit.

Because it is exceedingly unpleasant to take a walk through Paris against one's will accompanied by two guards marching you right to the top of the Rue de Clichy.[12]

---

[10] The Rue Saint-Honoré was a commercial street in the first arrondissement.

[11] The Palais-Royal and the Place de la Bourse are located in the first arrondissement, just steps away from each other. The Place Royale (today's Place des Vosges), on the other hand, is situated in the third arrondissement and is quite far away. Rue Greneta (misspelled in the original), also located in the second and third arrondissements, was known as a busy and somewhat unsavory commercial street.

[12] A reference to the location of a debtor's prison.

Chapter 3: Those Who Falsely
Claim to Be Flâneurs

People full of absurd ideas and presumptions can be found among all social classes. These individuals, abusing the French language in the most deplorable fashion, call themselves flâneurs not knowing the first thing about the leisurely art of flânerie that we hold in higher esteem than music, dance, or even mathematics.

There is much confusion in the matter: so many random individuals have usurped the title of *flâneur* for no reason whatsoever, as though it were a trivial matter. Thus the true flâneur, who rightfully joined the ranks of this eminently idle but deeply respected class, barely dares to admit he is a flâneur when he sees the most incoherent beings announce with utmost pretension: "I am a flâneur."

For example, on the Place Royale, you might encounter little old men busy frittering away their incomes who set out every day at noon from their homes under the pretext of going to practice flânerie. Ask them where they are going, and they will tell you in a jovial kind of tone—"I'm going to do some flânerie."

However, their flânerie consists of sitting down some twenty-five steps away from home. There they stay on a bench until dinnertime, in the company of one, two, or three friends and one, two, or three poodles. And for five hours, instead of walking, these fake flâneurs exercise their dogs with the help of a cane that is as useful as a Gisquet pistol;[13] but the cane is even more dangerous if it is loaded.

Then, after Azor, Castor, or Médor[14] has sufficiently run about, both dog and owner return home and announce with pride to the chambermaid, "We were just out practicing our flânerie."

Azor is really the one who deserves to be called "flâneur," because he is the one who drops the Gisquet-esque cane every now and then and goes off in search of an amorous encounter nearby.

When the rentier is ordered by his doctor to exercise, he enlists his friend Azor, so that his flânerie consists of dragging his leg while dragging a leash that drags the dog.

During the summer, these same old Frenchmen who boast of belonging to the wittiest nation in the universe engage in a different kind of flânerie. They run the

---

[13] A reference to a contemporary scandal involving the industrialist Henri Gisquet, who was tasked with purchasing several hundred thousand pistols for France, many of which proved defective.

[14] These are all common nineteenth-century names for pet dogs.

streets of the Marais and stop in every shop that sells melons. These men are mad for melons—what self-esteem!

Their flânerie consists in going from an orange cantaloupe to a green honeydew then back again to the cantaloupe. Finally, having sniffed the right one, our melon-head—no, I mean our man—finally decides to make his purchase and return home triumphantly with his trophy.

Sunday flâneurs also fall into the category of fake flâneurs: nothing less entertaining, or rather nothing more entertaining—because everything depends on your point of view—than the sight of a respectable but bored family strolling along the boulevards, from La Madeleine to the Bastille, on Sunday evening.

Yet, since the shops are closed on Sundays, their eyes only meet an uninterrupted row of green shutters, a sight that's healthy for the eyes, but monotonous for the mind.

This respectable paterfamilias, who has donned his best cornflower-colored suit to educate his wife and daughter in the pleasures of flânerie, forces them to exercise their jaws just as much as their legs.

That is the requisite portrait of all these little family flâneries.

Other Parisians, also paterfamilias, take pleasure in mocking these brave souls who are convinced they are

taking a leisurely stroll through the dust of the boulevards, and, so as not to fall victim to the same ridicule,
go every Sunday to practice flânerie on the hill of Montmartre instead.

Once they reach the top of the hill, they mop their
brows, remove their coats, loosen their ties, and sit gin-
gerly on a big stone.

Then, for three hours, they contemplate the dome
of the Invalides and the towers of Notre-Dame in the

distance—and they do the same thing fifty-two times a year, and each time with renewed pleasure.

Chapter 4: In Which We Prove That the Flâneur Is an Essentially Virtuous Mortal Being

I'm telling you the truth: if modern philanthropists are really dedicated to bettering mankind and getting rid of murder, theft, and all other dishonesties that many people still accept, instead of giving superb speeches and establishing poetry prizes for those authors who are best at praising virtue and vaccines, they would do much better to encourage, through all possible means, a taste for flânerie among all social classes.

I am not joking. My opinion is a respectable one, because it is a conscientious one. And it is certain that every man who strolls is a virtuous mortal. In order to completely adopt my way of seeing, it suffices to follow my reasoning for a few minutes and a few sentences.

What do those who stroll think about the most? "Nothing," you will say. That response is spot on, and by saying it you make a victorious argument in defense of my case.

If our flâneur is not thinking about anything, as you yourself have just admitted, he is not thinking about anything bad, and therefore, when this good, this truly excellent man comes toward you with his hands in his pockets, his nose in the air, you can be sure that he will not be a wicked ne'er-do-well contemplating the swiping of your snuffbox or the surreptitious removal of your scarf.

Not only is the flâneur not thinking about committing even the most minor of infractions, but you can bet that he has never in his life committed a transgression that has made the eyes of Justice look upon him, nor those of the city police for that matter.

A man with something to hide fears the sun and only comes out in the pale light of the gas lamps.[15] And if he has to run a few errands in Paris before sunset or before street lamps are lit, he slips furtively into the crowd, for he is scared of coming face to face with that other professional flâneur known as a police officer, whose special job is to detect suspicious traits in every single face he sees.

This head—topped with a three-cornered sergeant's hat—is a veritable Medusa for all guilty individuals. In fact, it is even more dangerous in the sense that, instead of just petrifying the unfortunate character, the officer's head is typically accompanied by a set of strong arms that can seize hold and not let go.

---

[15] Gas lighting was introduced in Paris beginning in 1812.

For that matter, even supposing that this individual had really pushed his Robert Macaire–like[16] swindling to the limits and that, for him, officers were nothing but simple mortals dressed in a more or less clean uniform, our guilty party could still find no pleasure in the pure joys of flânerie.

How is a man who has just committed a crime and is pondering his next one supposed to spend a delightful hour watching innocent children in the Tuileries garden and then spend another no less delightful and even more innocent sixty minutes watching the movements of the little goldfish in the ponds of the Tuileries?

It is impossible—truly of the utmost impossibility. What those half-wits need instead are even more mind-numbing pastimes. They prefer to stroll around the bars of wine-sellers' shops, making sure only to check out the *eau-de-vie*.[17]

----

[16] Robert Macaire was a popular stock character, an unscrupulous swindler. Created by the renowned actor Frédéric Lemaître in the 1820s, Macaire later appeared in a variety of works of popular culture. Best known among them are *Physiologie du Robert Macaire* (1842), written by Pierre-Joseph Rousseau and illustrated by Honoré Daumier, and a series of lithographs by Daumier featuring Macaire that appeared in the widely read satirical journal *Le charivari* between 1836 and 1842.

[17] Brandy made of fruit other than grapes.

Far from being an agent of theft, the flâneur is, on the contrary, often a victim of theft! What's more, Susse, Martinet, and Aubert[18] are often the innocent accomplices of a series of petty criminals who steal scarves for breakfast and snuffboxes for dinner.

It is terribly difficult to keep one's eyes on a caricature and one's pocket all at the same time—unless you can split them up and focus one eye on each of these two objects, but that's a nuisance and makes one seem appallingly cross-eyed.

So the flâneur must focus all of his attention and visual organs on the same store window. But then, while laughing at a Daumier caricature[19] that depicts one of the illustrious Macaire's great swindles, he is himself swindled out of a scarf and of all the accessories in his pocket, including his wallet. In the event that our flâneur is irritable or has a head cold, he flies into a dreadful rage against those individuals so perverse and unnatural that they would steal their peer's scarves. He hopes the guilty

---

[18] Susse and Aubert were publishers of popular, often satirical texts. Martinet was a contemporary lithographer. A large number of *physiologies* were published by Aubert.

[19] Honoré Daumier was a French artist, illustrator, and caricaturist especially known for his biting social satire and commentary. Daumier illustrated many of the *physiologies*, including *Physiology of the Flâneur*.

party will receive the severest punishments—even the guillotine seems like too weak a punishment in that first moment.

As a result, the flâneur has not even the slightest pity for the thieves who are arrested. If the guilty party were to escape by tripping up Justice and the officer, our flâneur would be capable of going after him like a vulgar policeman. That's how big a grudge he still holds about his missing scarf.

The moral of the story: all flâneurs are virtuous mortals.

Chapter 7: The Pavement Pounder

Are you under the impression that flânerie is just for civil servants, rentiers, lawyers without cases, infantry soldiers — in a word, men of leisure? Do you think that flânerie is a distraction for everyone, a way to pass the time, as it is for you? Well, that would be a misunderstanding of the industrious nature of your century, an insult to the intelligence of your fellow citizens.

Certainly, in a developed country such as our own—in a city where water, air, fire, land, love, honor, wit, body, and soul are all sold, rented, and exploited in every possible way—flânerie should be put to use in some fashion. It should offer, for example, a way for a few individuals to levy a tax on the many: the philosophical goal on which civilization's progress is always premised.

From this theory of political economy, the Pavement Pounder is born. This species is diverse. It is a class with a wealth of needs, an especially respectable class when it comes to its size. In Paris alone it is made up of those thirty thousand consumers who get up each morning without knowing how they will dine or where they will sleep. This problem, in accordance with the theory of probability, has the following solution:

> Dinner: At the expense of others
> Lodging: Ditto

But, on particularly terrible days, the problem usually resolves itself in the following way:

> Dinner: None
> Lodging: In the slammer

It would take too long to tell you all the nuances of this species and would take more work than either of us is willing to do: too much for me to write and too much for you to read. So let's just pick some of the most remarkable traits.

That intimate friend you do not know, but whom you encounter in every public place, who always smiles at you, who shakes your hand, and who finishes up the day—or rather starts it—by borrowing twenty francs from you—that's a Pavement Pounder!

That man who runs into a boutique, seeming very busy, and says to the bonnet-maker or haberdasher whose name he has just read on the sign: "My God! Monsieur Barnabé, I am your neighbor. I live right over here at number 26. I made a little purchase, and I'm just five francs short. I don't want to run back up to my place. Would you please lend them to me?" That's a Pavement Pounder!

That man with decent comportment and a venerable air, who sports a red ribbon and a bald head—he is the unofficial collector of charities for victims of the flood, the fire, and all other trendy calamities—that's a Pavement Pounder! Your alms will go straight from his hands to those of the croupier in the gambling den.

This Polish man from Strasbourg, this Spaniard from Pézenas,[20] this Neapolitan from Turin: all these contraband foreign nobles who appeal to your magnanimity—all are Pavement Pounders!

And that poor devil—filthy, tatty, ruined—who worriedly glances at the posters in restaurants:

---

[20] Pézenas is a commune in the Hérault department in the Occitan region in southern France.

DINNER FOR 17 SOUS
Three courses, a small carafe
of wine, and a dessert

DINNER FOR 23 SOUS
Four courses of your choice, half
a bottle of wine from Mâcon,
dessert, and unlimited bread

—and who, given that he is missing change for both the 17-sou and the 23-sou dinner, starts looking for it in the pockets of strangers, either in front of the stands of print dealers or in the crowds of the Museum or at the Punch and Judy street stage or in any other meeting of gawkers—that's another Pavement Pounder! That particular one is called a pocket-puller.

We also have the *bonjourien*, who pounds the pavement at eight o'clock in the morning, scouring houses, entering where he can enter, taking everything he can take, and leaving while wishing you *bonjour* and apologizing for having woken you up.

Then there's the *American*, who strolls at all hours trying to find a sack on the back of a gullible fool, to whom he jabbers about trading two crowns for one golden guinea—a trade that the fool accepts, either out of greed or stupidity, and in turn receives, for his good money, either lead, gilded pennies, or rolled tokens.

Finally, in the same category, we find the nocturnal flâneur, the modest flower of large cities, who can handle neither the sun's light nor that of the lampposts, and who only blossoms in the shade of solitary streets or, if you'll permit me the botanical pun, in the hothouses of the police station.

But the Pavement Pounder par excellence is that philosopher who lives happily from hand to mouth, without luxury, without shame, without expecting to be rich, without bias, making do with all that everyone else rejects, not eating much, drinking a lot, and able to exclaim, like Bias,

Omnia mecum porto![21]

In a word, it's the working-class flâneur, the king of the pavement, the French ragpicker.

Chapter 8: The Perfect Flâneur

Good legs, good ears, and good eyes: these are the main physical attributes that all Frenchmen deserving of membership in the flâneur club must possess (when one is formed . . . which really must happen soon).

---

[21] The saying "Omnia mea mecum porto" 'All that is mine I take with me' is attributed to the ancient Greek sage Bias of Priene and the Roman philosopher Cicero. Here the Pavement Pounder says, "I take everything with me."

Good legs are necessary for strolling along all the promenades, all the sidewalks, all the quays, all the squares, all the boulevards of Paris. Good ears are for not missing any of the witty remarks (or the pleasantly stupid ones) that can be heard in all the groups that typically come together in public spaces. Finally, good eyes are required in order to notice all the lovely women sellers, all the hideous faces, all the baroque signs, and all the dainty legs that one comes across over the course of a flânerie.

The paletot jacket[22] seems to have been invented especially for the flâneur. Thanks to this practical item—cut in the shape of a sack—the flâneur can calmly put his two hands in his pockets and slip through the thickest of crowds, even the ones full of seedy characters, without fear that a nosy neighbor will be tempted to plumb the depths of these same pockets. The paletot jacket reduces pickpocketing tremendously—pickpocketing being the name of the practice that consists of picking scarves, snuffboxes, opera glasses, and other items from all the pockets. It is true that if the paletot jacket has largely cut down on pickpocketing, it has by contrast greatly increased the number of thefts complemented by

----

[22] A short, loose overcoat for men, introduced in the nineteenth century.

murder. Industrious thieves no longer find themselves obligated to completely strip the nocturnal flâneur of his possessions, since they can simply see what he has in his pockets. But since they start the process by strangling or knocking out their chosen subject, it becomes clear that if the paletot jacket has its charms, it also has its drawbacks.

There are perhaps only three social groups in which one can find hearts and legs truly worthy of belonging to a flâneur. These three groups are made up of poets, artists, and law clerks.

When I say *poets*, I do not mean making rhyming epics or love poems, like the nosegays to Cloris.[23] I mean having poetry or heart—that even rarer quality that cannot be found in the *Dictionary of Rhymes*—and also imagination.

The flâneur makes up an entire novel from a mere trifle, like meeting a woman on the omnibus, her face covered with a veil. One minute later, he engages in the highest philosophical, social, and humanitarian considerations by admiring all the miracles that education can confer on the absent-minded young men who engage in duels like a real-life Saint George.[24]

---

[23] A short romantic verse aimed at seducing the interlocutor.
[24] Saint George is associated with the myth of dragon slaying.

Artists are even more flâneur-like, because for them, the strolling is a real necessity. Once you've spent five hours in your office or at your easel, you get even more pleasure from playing hooky after work, although sometimes you also want to do it before work.

Then, because they can easily get into all the theaters, artists engage in a particular type of flânerie. They either eye the whole audience from the orchestra seats or go dancing cancans backstage with all the young *rats*.[25] God knows that the backstage is the refuge of all the gossipy *rats*, especially at the Opera.

Then, at eleven o'clock, instead of going to sleep like a vulgar national guardsman, the flâneur makes a little stop in one of the many cafés where you can enjoy Gros-Caillou oriental tobacco.[26] Then, finally, the flâneur can be perfectly happy! Because instead of dreaming about fortunes or wars, cats or dogs, he dreams . . . about the Marche du Boeuf Gras, the Descente de la Cortille,[27] indeed any procession—at any rate, he is dreaming about flânerie!

---

[25] Like the flâneur, the *rat*, a young female dancer at the Paris Opera, was a recognizable urban type.

[26] Situated in the seventh arrondissement, Gros-Caillou was the site of a large tobacco factory.

[27] The main processions during the Paris Carnival.

Henry Monnier

Physiology of the Bourgeois

Henry Monnier was a notable figure of nineteenth-century popular culture who worked as a writer, lithographer, and actor.

Chapter 1: What Is a Bourgeois?

Let's agree on one thing and proceed accordingly. Our Bourgeois is not the same as yours, nor is he the same as your neighbor's. He is neither the soldier's Bourgeois nor the peasant's. Just as no two snowflakes are alike, I don't see why it wouldn't be the same for the Bourgeois.

The soldier's Bourgeois is anyone who does not wear a uniform: a real one, not the fake dress-up uniform of the National Guard, with a horse and red trousers.[1] During the Empire, the soldier called the Bourgeois "Peking silk"[2] and constantly threatened to cut his ears off with a big sword. It was fashionable at the time, and one had

---

[1] The national guard was first formed during the French Revolution in 1792 as a *milice bourgeoise* ("bourgeois militia"). It was firmly associated with the interests of the middle class. Here Monnier derisively opposes the national guard to "real" soldiers.

[2] *Étoffe pékin* is a kind of silk that was mostly made in France in imitation of Chinese silk. "Pequin" was also a term that soldiers under Napoleon used to deride the bourgeois, meaning "civilian" or "civvy."

to conform. Today, the Bourgeois is quite fond of his ears, and he preserves them with great care. Nature has many tastes, and this one is certainly quite respectable. There is nothing depraved about it.

The peasant's Bourgeois is a city dweller who carries a brown coat under one arm and a bowler hat under another, and wears shirts with collars, embroidered ties, nankeen cotton,[3] and silk gloves. Generally speaking, the peasant cannot stand the urbanite who comes every Sunday to humiliate him by showing off the luxury of his dress and his fancy outfit. And so, every time the peasant encounters the Bourgeois, he quickly seizes the opportunity to beat the living daylights out of him, making sure that there are always four against one. You can't fail to admire the simplicity, the unceremonious nature of country manners.

The worker who lives in the city knows but one, the only one: the Bourgeois of the workshop. That's his own Bourgeois, or, if you prefer, his master, his boss.

True gentlemen, if you're even willing to admit that they still exist, disdainfully understand *Bourgeois* to mean all those little people who wear the best-quality fabric (the same fabric worn by counts and marquises, but

---

[3] This term refers to a yellow cotton fabric, originally produced in Nanjing, frequently called Nanking, China. In the nineteenth century, nankeen was produced in Europe.

often worn better by the Bourgeois) but who themselves are not *well born*, even if they are sometimes seventy or eighty years old.

There is also bourgeois comedy, bourgeois dining, bourgeois cuisine—but let's leave things aside and return to people.

For drivers of carriages for hire, the Bourgeois is any individual who boards his vehicle, be it a municipal guard with all his weapons and luggage or a simple urchin in overalls and a cap. Besides, thanks to his independence (the best advantage of his profession), the driver would be embarrassed to say *my Bourgeois*. He says *our Bourgeois*, which makes a big difference. Saying *my Bourgeois* would indicate that he recognizes himself to be your driver, your humble servant, whereas he only admits that you're the Bourgeois of all other drivers the moment you thought of boarding a carriage. The proof of what I propose here is that the moment you descend from the carriage or, to use the driver's language, the moment you're *unloaded*, he will splatter you from head to toe while yelling, "Watch out, you animal!" Which certainly proves that he has ceased to consider you a Bourgeois.

With artists, it's totally different. The word *Bourgeois* is not a name, a meaning, a title; it's an insult, and the most vulgar one that can be found in an artist's studio.

An artist's apprentice would prefer a thousand times over to be called the most heinous names rather than be called a Bourgeois. It is in the painter's studio that he behaves particularly harshly toward the Bourgeois. The Bourgeois in the artist's studio is in especially grave danger, like a creditor in the debtor's prison. Moreover, today's artist is just as exclusive in the way he considers the Bourgeois as the soldier was in 1808, because he considers a Bourgeois anyone who is not associated with his family, and treats them with no pity.

As for the Bourgeois himself, according to the national guard, he is defined as a man with a good three to four thousand livres in income, who does not owe anything to anyone, who enjoys a good meal, and who floats down the river of life with warm feet, cotton balls in his ears, and a cane in hand.

There is not a single merchant, haberdasher, ironmonger, knickknack maker, or even grocer who does not dream of this happy and easy bourgeois existence for his later years.

If you don't mind, lovely reader, we are going to tackle the Bourgeois from all sides, and we will call by this name any individual who, through his tastes, habits, tics, and style appears to have the right to this title. We will review all types and varieties of this immense and fascinating family.

Chapter 2: His Birth, Education, and Early Years

What a strange thing! The Bourgeois appears to have come into the world at the age of fifty, with gray hair, glasses, a big belly, a black outfit, and white stockings. If you want to understand him, it's then or never. When he is younger, he is not mature or developed enough. It would be too much trouble to analyze him. He really amounts to nothing. As a child, he was a prodigy. When asked, "How is your daddy doing, my little friend?" he would answer at once and without hesitation, "Rue Charlot, no. 45, in the Marais."

"And your mommy, is she still in the countryside?"

"Rue Charlot, no. 45, in the Marais."

"Will she be coming back soon?"

"Rue Charlot, no. 45, in the Marais."

To each new question, he would respond with his address. It was impossible to take advantage of him. It was utterly baffling. As a result, he would be left alone, which was certainly the best solution.

If his daddy—the same one who was inquired about—had the misfortune of making a mistake (which happened quite often, because for the life of him the poor dear man could not pronounce a name without butchering it), the little boy would immediately set him on the right path, which greatly displeased his forebear. But there was nothing to be said. His mommy found him charming and bestowed endearing names upon him: her *darling treasure*; her *god of love*; her *little chickadee*; her *sweet prince*. She covered him with the sweetest tears and with the tenderest of caresses.

At the age of five, he recites the fable "The Crow and the Fox"[4] during dessert; later on, he reviews kings and queens of France, princes and princesses, streets and intersections, markets and stalls, administrative centers, the year, the day, and the hour when Joshua, who stopped the sun, left this valley of misery and tears for a better world.[5] At the age of eighteen, he finishes his studies, having obtained honors. He knows Greek and Latin *ex professo*[6] but has not the slightest idea about spelling and is profoundly ignorant about even basic good manners. He talks with his mouth full, he places his elbows on the table. He is, in a word, quite a sad subject, a naughty little monkey.

The Bourgeois ordinarily possesses beautiful handwriting, thanks to Monsieur his father, who drilled it into his head from early childhood that you have to eat boiled

---

[4] A fable by Jean de La Fontaine.

[5] Joshua is a central character in the Hebrew Bible. He was Moses's assistant and became leader of the Israelites after Moses's death. During the battle with the Amorite kings at Gibeon, Joshua commanded the sun to stand still so that he could finish the battle in daylight.

[6] As an expert.

meat and bread with every meal, and that with beautiful handwriting you will succeed at everything—which is an error, and a grave one at that. My apologies to anyone who shares this opinion. It is, on the contrary, a misfortune in many circumstances, and a big one—the biggest one that can happen to a young man—to have beautiful handwriting. Without making a mountain out of a molehill, consider the fate reserved to those with beautiful handwriting in administration. What becomes of them? They become forwarding agents.[7] People with beautiful handwriting are so rare that when you have them, you keep them. This is the case with all those who have beautiful handwriting, whatever their career: pharmacy, lithography, metallurgy, or diplomacy. Thus, unless he is born on a throne or something, rarely does beautiful handwriting do the Bourgeois any good.

Chapter 5: The Mania of Portraits. His Relationship with Artists.

When the Bourgeois doesn't know how to spend his time in a more appropriate manner, he gets himself "done." This is one of his principal occupations, a veritable mania, a need. This urge to be painted is felt particularly acutely as the weather gets warmer. Since he's sprucing

---

[7] Clerks who arrange the shipment of goods.

up his lodging, he may as well spruce himself up while the painters are at it. If he has his apartment repainted, he also orders new portraits of himself, so that the old ones don't clash with the wall's new colors.

Madame has the portrait of her husband; Monsieur has the portrait of Madame: twenty, thirty of them, sometimes more. It's endless. They decorate their cane knobs, their parasol and umbrella covers. They adorn their chests and bellies, their jabots and their collars. There is not a single corner in the apartment that is not inundated. Even in places where you would least expect to find a work of art, you'll find one or several portraits of the master of the house.

The silhouette, and later the daguerreotype,[8] were previously used to represent some of these gentlemen. But the majority of the subjects found themselves so ugly and so dark that they have abandoned this medium.

Ever since sculpture descended from its high pedestal and began to run the streets, the Bourgeois has added a new passion to his arsenal. So his unfortunate physique has been exploited in all possible ways: as a medallion, a bust, and a statuette. And he has not stopped there. He

---

[8] This technique, in which an image is recorded on a silvered copper plate, was introduced by Louis-Jacques-Mandé Daguerre in 1839 and remained the most successful commercial photographic process until 1860.

has had his arm, his leg, his nose, and his ears sculpted. The only thing he didn't want is his caricature. But due to artists' indiscretions, his caricature has been exhibited in the windows of fashionable stores, alongside contemporary celebrities.

You might well think, from the Bourgeois's behavior, that he wishes to win back the artist's esteem by all means possible. But if this is his intention, he rarely succeeds. Even if we admit that he wants to build a rapport, which I seriously doubt, the artist would hardly agree to this. The former does not grasp the mission of the latter, while the latter understands the former even less. There is more: even though both speak the same language, they do not understand each other. The artist is negatively predisposed toward the Bourgeois, and the Bourgeois feels the same way about the artist. So their interactions are inevitably unpleasant—yet they keep interacting. What's even more deplorable is that one of them pays and the other one gets paid. The one who's buying gives himself license to make comments that are rarely well received by the one who sells.

It is always the same motivation that leads the Bourgeois to the artist's studio: the desire to please his spouse by preparing a surprise for her yet again; or vanity; or, as we have already said, a desire to be refreshed. So, one fine morning, he barges into the studio of an artist recommended to him or whose work he saw at an acquaintance's house.

"Monsieur," says the Bourgeois in a friendly voice, opening the door as our story begins, "do you know me?"

"Not yet, monsieur," responds the artist in a minimally mocking tone, "but I would be delighted to make your acquaintance."

"Do you paint?"

"Yes, monsieur."

"Portraits?"

"Yes, monsieur. Please have a seat."

"Never mind that. In color?"

"Yes, Monsieur."

"Like the one of Tabarot?"

"You know Monsieur Tabarot?"

"Do I know him? Indeed! What a strange question. We are married to sisters. He is my brother-in-law. He was the one who told me about you. He knows you are not happy, and he will do everything he can to please you, you can rest assured."

"Monsieur Tabarot is a good man."

"Ah, yes, and often to people who don't deserve it. He is the best thing since sliced bread, that good old Tabarot, incapable of saying no to anyone. But you made him too red."

"Is that so?"

"Indeed! I am sure of it, he is much too red. It's much too much. Tabarot has never been so red. Listen, be fair, don't you agree he is too red?"

"I don't know. But he did seem to have a bit of color, Monsieur Tabarot."

"But of course he does. If he didn't, it would be very sad for all who know him. But he is not red to that extent, come on! It defies common sense. You made him beet red. But listen, I want a portrait of me painted as soon as possible."

"Right away, if you wish."

"I'll take you at your word. All the same, despite what you say, Tabarot is far too red. If he weren't so red, he'd be perfect, but he is not. Where should I sit?"

"Wherever you like."

"How about here, in this corner? I like to be as far from the light as possible. Bright light bothers me."

"But it's too dark there."

"Don't worry, it will be fine. What position should I take?"

"Whatever you wish. Sit in whatever position is typical for you."

"Maybe reading a book?"

"Why not?"

"Do you have a book?"

"Here is one."

"What is it?"

"Voltaire, *The Age of Louis XIV*."

"Voltaire, I like him well enough. He drank a lot of coffee. That fellow had a lot of money, and yet it didn't keep him from dying. I have all his books in my library, but I never read them. I can't read for more than five minutes without falling asleep. It often happens to me while reading—that's the problem."

"Your book hides half of your face."

"Really? Is this better?"

And our chap, already feeling the aforementioned effect, lets his chin droop to his chest and his eyes blink shut, whistles like a seal, and forces the artist to yell, "Monsieur!" (*riforzando*)[9] "MONSIEUR!"

"Ah! Ah! Here I am!"

"Your head is too low."

"You're right, this position will make the blood rush to my head. You will make me as red as Tabarot. Do you prefer it this way?"

"Your head is a bit too high."

"Well, I don't know what you want. I have another good pose in mind. But I usually only make it in the winter. It's when I warm myself up."

---

[9] Usually *rinforzando*; a musical term denoting a swell in volume or a sudden forcefulness.

"Let's see it."

"How do you find it?"

"It's pretty good, but your face is completely hidden. Unless you want to have yourself painted from the back."

"At home, that would not be a problem. You would be behind me and could see me in the mirror. Oh, well, so anyway, where would you like me to sit?"

"Why don't you stay right where you are?"

"I couldn't ask for anything better. But let's get this moving already."

"Now you're perfect."

"Above all, don't make me red. I am not red. It's not the first time that I have myself painted, thank you very much!"

"You've already had yourself painted?"

"Goodness me, yes. I have had my portrait done, and that of my spouse many times! Look, it's on my snuffbox, you see? On my shirt, in my wallet. I have it everywhere. Isn't it pretty? It's a Bibochet; have you already seen the Bibochets?"[10]

"Not yet."

"You've never seen his work?"

"Never."

---

[10] Here Bibochet is the name of a fictitious artist and also refers to a stock character who appears in several popular texts.

"He was famous. He was so popular. Everyone wanted to have themselves 'done' by Bibochet. Everyone swore by him. He cost me a pretty penny."

"He was not expensive."

"He did it so fast! There was always a line at his studio. He earned quite a bit of gold, that Bibochet, which didn't keep him from dying at the hospital for the poor. And yet they said he was a respectable man. But he never wanted to do anything. He was disorganized, like all you people: a leaky basket with holes."

"Monsieur . . ."

"Look, be fair, and don't get angry. Admit that what you're doing here is not a proper profession, and if you are doing it, it's against your parents' wishes. Be honest."

"Not at all."

"In that case, I don't understand them . . . I just can't sit still . . . I could never do it . . . It always has the same effect on me when I have myself 'done' . . . I can't help myself . . . it puts me to sleep . . ."

And in fact, after five minutes, the Bourgeois is asleep!

Chapter 11: The Bourgeois at the Theater

There is nothing sadder than sitting next to a Bourgeois at the theater, especially if you're in the box seats. You have paid a lot of money to spend the most exhausting and laborious evening imaginable. For five or six hours, you will shoulder the burden of a gentleman weighing 75 kilograms physically and 250 kilograms morally.

The theatergoing Bourgeois falls into two general categories: the Bourgeois who adores everything, and the Bourgeois who loathes everything. Frankly, it is hard to tell which one is worse.

The enthusiastic Bourgeois explodes with joy every two seconds, which, in the end, will make you dislike even the acting of Arnal himself,[11] if such a thing were possible.

Every minute, he elbows his neighbor to tell him:

"A great play, don't you think?"

"Excellent actors, right?"

"Could I possibly ask you, Monsieur, who is the author of this play?"

"And this actor, the one with the big nose, who is he, please? Would you be so kind as to tell me his name, please?"

"Thanks a million, Monsieur."

"Pardon me, this actress, isn't she Madame . . . I have her name on the tip of my tongue . . . Madame ***?"

---

[11] Étienne Arnal was a French comic actor.

"No, Monsieur, she is at the Opéra-Comique. We are at the Ambigu," etc, etc.[12]

If misfortune has it that the neighbor has already seen the play, it's simply impossible to be seated next to him. He sings the songs with the actors, he blurts out all the lines like a stage prompter. As soon as the curtain goes down, the torture, far from being over, only increases. Because the Bourgeois, who paid to enjoy himself the entire evening, will do anything to achieve this goal. He questions you and calls out to you as if you were old pals. If he doesn't demand your name and address, don't be too grateful; it's just that it does not occur to him. It's not for lack of encouragement on his part. He tells you his first and last name, his age, his profession, his tastes, his habits, his political and literary opinions, as well as other things that he could have very well kept to himself, such as, for example, that he likes spinach but prefers endives.

This gentleman is polite; he eagerly offers you tobacco (even though you declined the very first time he offered). If he steps on your foot, which he does at every inter-mission, he apologizes so profusely, he offers so many excuses, that you cannot possibly hold a grudge. It is only

---

[12] The Opéra-Comique and the Théâtre de l'Ambigu-Comique were popular Parisian theaters.

at the end of the performance, after the four-hundred-and-eighty-seventh question, that you can allow yourself to respond, "Monsieur, you are infuriating!"

Well, perhaps you will miss this neighbor if, the next day, your unlucky star lands you upon, or rather next to, a Bourgeois who finds everything terrible.

This gentleman, who is ordinarily of a certain age and is suffering from rheumatism, his head adorned with a blond or black toupee, does not address a single word to you, does not apologize in the least when he steps all over you, and does not stop mumbling nonsense from the very first moments of the play until the end. He rails against the actors, the musicians, the ushers who leave the door open and subject him to a draft of cold air; he rails against gas lighting, against air heaters, against the cabbage he ate for dinner, and against himself, for having the terrible idea of coming to the theater in the first place.

"Ah! You call this a great actor?" he says about a popular performer. "This is the man everyone thinks is so funny? He doesn't even make me crack a smile. He is most ordinary. It's just terrible—he is a tightrope walker, a clown, a wretch!"

"This woman is repulsive. She has a reputation for being beautiful, but she is hideous, without any grace or demeanor. She says everything wrong. Ah! Good heavens!"

"And this orchestra that makes so much noise! For God's sake, don't play so loudly, you wretches! You're butchering our ears! How awful; you might as well throw all those people out the window. And this play, what does it mean anyway? Where did they find these characters, all these silly people, huh? It's dreadful."

What's most unfortunate about sitting next to such an individual is that it's impossible to respond to him. Because he would tell you, very reasonably, that *he is not talking to you!*

That was a Bourgeois bachelor. As for the Bourgeois who is married with children, who goes to the theater only about three times a year, accompanied by his wife, his maid, and his five little ones, he is naturally eight times more annoying.

The Bourgeois enthusiastically seeks to become acquainted with an actor, and even more so with an author, because this raises his hopes of going to the theater for free. And if indeed he does get so-called complimentary tickets, he must pay one franc for the rights of the poor, a second franc for the destitute, and a third as a surcharge. So for three francs, he gets a balcony seat that costs a mere thirty-five centimes at the ticket office. It is true that the ushers treat him with arrogance, and the attendants threaten to call the police if he continues to complain.

Authors rarely give this sort of complimentary ticket to their friends, unless these friends tried to flirt with their wives and they wish to avenge themselves.

You have to give credit to the Bourgeois: he always asks for such tickets in a very particular manner. "My dear friend, can you get me into so-and-so's play tonight? It's supposed to be charming. You should adopt his style; it is so much more sophisticated than yours."

Or else, if he knows a comedic author, he will ask him for two tickets, adding with the aplomb and self-assurance that is typical of people of his kind, "It's not for me; I would never see these types of plays. It's for my maid, whose sister is visiting."

And the author is supposed to be happy to do something that would please the Bourgeois's maid and her sister!

Otherwise, when the Bourgeois runs into his theater acquaintances on the street, he will turn his head away so that he doesn't have to greet them, for fear of being spotted by his boss or a captain of the national guard. He would not be happy if it became known that he frequents minstrels or street artists.

Others are not as proud and, on the contrary, are charmed to know famous actors. One of these gentlemen even had the following printed on his calling cards: VERDELET, FRIEND OF BERNARD-LÉON.[13] He would tell anybody who came along what time his old friend went to bed, what time he ate, his tastes, his habits, his tailor's address, and that of his hatmaker, the name of his boss, his age, and his birthday. Some people are unscrupulous enough to get things at another's expense, and then they tear into them with criticism. This is actually pretty common.

---

[13] Jean-Pierre Bernard, known as Bernard-Léon, was a French actor, theater director, and playwright.

Works Cited in Headnotes and Footnotes

Bara, Olivier. "Dérive, déliaison, délire: du scenario vaudevillesque au calembour 'à l'Odry.'" *Le rire modern*, PU de Paris Ouest, 2013, pp. 377–92.

Benjamin, Walter. *The Arcades Project*. Translated by Howard Eiland and Kevin McLaughlin, The Belknap Press, 2002.

Brown, Marilyn R. *The Gamin de Paris in Nineteenth-Century Visual Culture: Delacroix, Hugo, and the French Social Imaginary*. Routledge, 2017.

D'Souza, Aruna, and Tom McDonough, editors. *The Invisible Flâneuse? Gender, Public Space, and Visual Culture in Nineteenth-Century Paris*. Manchester UP, 2006.

Ferguson, Priscilla. "The Flâneur on and off the Streets of Paris." *The Flâneur*, edited by Keith Tester, Routledge, 1994, pp. 22–42.

———. *Paris as Revolution: Writing the Nineteenth-Century City*. U of California P, 1994.

Hiner, Susan. *Accessories to Modernity: Fashion and the Feminine in Nineteenth-Century France*. U of Pennsylvania P, 2010.

Kessler, Marni. *Sheer Presence: The Veil in Manet's Paris*. U of Minnesota P, 2006.

La Fontaine, Jean de. *Joconde*. *Œuvres complètes de La Fontaine*, vol. 1, Hachette et Cie, 1861, pp. 293–305.

Leff, Lisa Moses. "Eugénie Foa." *The Encyclopedia of Jewish Women*, jwa.org/encyclopedia/article/foa-eugenie.

Marcus, Sharon. *Apartment Stories: City and Home in Nineteenth-Century Paris and London*. U of California P, 1999.

Nead, Lynda. *The Victorian Babylon: People, Streets and Images in Nineteenth-Century London*. Yale UP, 2000.

Nesci, Catherine. *Le flâneur et les flâneuses. Les femmes et la ville à l'époque romantique*. Ellug, 2007.

Robb, Graham. *Victor Hugo: A Biography*. W. W. Norton, 1999.

Sainte-Beuve, Charles-Augustin. "De la littérature industrielle." *Revue des deux mondes*, vol. 4, no. 19, 1839, pp. 675–91.

Simond, Charles, editor. *La vie parisienne à travers le xixe siècle. Paris de 1800 à 1900 d'après les estampes et les mémoires du temps publié*. Plon, 1901.